"*The Negative Thoughts Workbook* offers a plethora of excellent, evidence-based, and well-presented strategies to address repetitive negative thinking related to anxiety and depression. If you engage in this type of thinking—and we all do from time to time—this book will help you to recognize your thought patterns and implement effective ways to change them. Written in an engaging and practical style by one of the world's experts in the psychology of negative thinking, you will benefit from reading this book and using the skills it offers."

—**Keith S. Dobson, PhD**, professor of clinical psychology at the University of Calgary, and president of the World Confederation of Cogniti̶ ̶ ̶ ̶ ̶d Behavioural Therapies

"Repetitive negative thoughts can be distressing, and interfere with our daily lives. In this excellent and clearly written workbook, David Clark gives you concrete strategies and practical solutions to deal with worry, rumination, regret, shame, humiliation, and resentment. This masterfully written and resourceful book will change your life. A must-read."

—**Stefan G. Hofmann, PhD**, professor at Boston University, and author of *The Anxiety Skills Workbook*

"If you are struggling with repetitive negative thoughts causing anxiety, depression, regret, shame, guilt, humiliation, anger, or resentment, this clearly written and practical workbook can really help. As a world-renowned psychologist and researcher, David Clark integrates a range of cognitive-behavioral approaches to provide you with an effective, step-by-step guide to help you overcome repetitive negative thoughts. I will certainly be recommending this workbook to my patients, students, and colleagues."

—**Costas Papageorgiou, DClinPsy, PhD**, coauthor of *Coping with Depression*, and coeditor of *Depressive Rumination*

"Here is an outstanding guide that helps people find freedom from the painful thoughts that make life miserable. David Clark—one of the most knowledgeable and esteemed experts of our time—distills the essentials into a single book. This is a comprehensive course that teaches you leading-edge approaches to free your mind from disturbing thoughts and emotions. I consider it essential reading for all those with a 'sticky' mind."

—**Martin N. Seif, PhD, ABPP**, founder of the Anxiety and Depression Association of America (ADAA), and coauthor of *What Every Therapist Needs to Know About Anxiety Disorders, Overcoming Unwanted Intrusive Thoughts*, and *Needing to Know for Sure*

"Following a negative life experience, most of us have had the experience of reliving the event in our minds, wondering why it happened and whether life will ever be the same. This repetitive negative thought process only serves to fuel emotional pain and suffering. Using thought-provoking exercises and illustrative case examples, *The Negative Thoughts Workbook* by David Clark teaches readers how to interrupt rumination and use effective strategies to move beyond disappointment, regret, and resentment. This book is extremely readable, and offers countless techniques that readers can tackle independently without the guidance of a therapist. It is a fantastic resource for anyone wanting to worry less and live a more productive, meaningful life in the present moment."

—**Deborah Roth Ledley, PhD**, licensed psychologist in private practice in Philadelphia, PA; and coauthor of *The Worry Workbook for Kids*

"David Clark is a go-to expert in understanding and overcoming negative thoughts. In this book, he brings together his scholarship and clinical experience to create an easy-to-use and highly effective guide to dealing with a wide range of negative thoughts that can otherwise plague our mood and ability to get things done. Highly recommended!"

—**Christine Purdon, PhD, CPsych**, professor in the department of psychology at the University of Waterloo, and coauthor of *Overcoming Obsessive Thoughts*

"This is a timely and important book for those with anxiety and depression issues. It is increasingly recognized that dealing with rumination, worry, and shame is important to these and other problems. David Clark has worldwide recognition as a leading therapist, and has published widely in this academic area. He has used these skills in developing an accessible and helpful workbook that I would recommend to clients and therapists alike."

—**Richard Moulding, PhD**, senior lecturer at Deakin University in Australia, editor in chief of *Clinical Psychologist*, and coeditor of *The Self in Understanding and Treating Psychological Disorders*

"Instead of writing one or several books on anxiety, depression, guilt, anger, or other distressing emotions, David Clark takes us to what is behind these emotions: namely repetitive negative thinking like worry or rumination. Using the principles of cognitive behavioral therapy (CBT), and excellent and handy worksheets and exercises—and in a very kind, user friendly, step-by-step way—Clark helps us get rid of repetitive negative thoughts and related feelings."

—**Gregoris Simos, MD, PhD**, professor of psychopathology in the department of educational and social policy at the University of Macedonia in Greece

"David Clark's *The Negative Thoughts Workbook* is one of the most lucid and accessible workbooks I have seen. Solidly based in the latest scientific evidence, this workbook by one of the world's leading experts provides the reader with the information, self-assessment tools, and step-by-step exercises that can help them to get more control over feelings of anxiety, depression, obsessive-compulsive disorder (OCD), and other emotional problems."

—**John H. Riskind, PhD**, professor of psychology at George Mason University, and coauthor of *Looming Vulnerability*

The Negative Thoughts Workbook

CBT Skills to Overcome the
Repetitive Worry, Shame, and Rumination
That Drive Anxiety and Depression

• • • • • •

DAVID A. CLARK, PhD

New Harbinger Publications, Inc.

Publisher's Note

NEW HARBINGER PUBLICATIONS is a registered trademark of New Harbinger Publications, Inc.

New Harbinger Publications is an employee-owned company.

Distributed in Canada by Raincoast Books

Cover design by Amy Daniel; Acquired by Ryan Buresh; Edited by Gretel Hakanson

---

Library of Congress Cataloging-in-Publication Data

Names: Clark, David A., 1954- author.
Title: The negative thoughts workbook : CBT skills to overcome the repetitive worry, shame, and rumination that drive anxiety and depression / David A. Clark.
Description: Oakland, CA : New Harbinger Publications, [2020] | Includes bibliographical references.
Identifiers: LCCN 2020013661 (print) | LCCN 2020013662 (ebook) | ISBN 9781684035052 (trade paperback) | ISBN 9781684035076 (epub) | ISBN 9781684035069 (pdf)
Subjects: LCSH: Intrusive thoughts. | Anxiety--Prevention. | Affective disorders. | Cognitive therapy.
Classification: LCC RC531 .C536 2020 (print) | LCC RC531 (ebook) | DDC 616.85/22--dc23
LC record available at https://lccn.loc.gov/2020013661
LC ebook record available at https://lccn.loc.gov/2020013662

Printed in the United States of America

25	24	23				
10	9	8	7	6	5	4

Contents

Foreword

Is your mind hijacked by intrusive repetitive negative thoughts? Perhaps you worry that things will fall apart, that you won't get that work done, that your boss will be angry at you, or that your plane may crash. You may find yourself losing sleep because you worry that you will lose sleep—and then you worry that you won't be able to function the next day. Or perhaps your repetitive negative thoughts (RNT) focus on past mistakes, mishaps, poor choices, or regrets that seem to follow you around no matter how well things are going today. You are anchored to the past—to these ruminations that creep into your troubled mind and deprive you of the ability to enjoy the present moment. No need to worry any further because this book will help you let go of the thoughts that plague you while you focus on solving real problems in real time in the real world.

David A. Clark is an eminent cognitive behavioral psychologist whose research on anxiety and depression is world-class. But he is also a gifted clinician who is able to write for the general public in a highly accessible and sensible manner. This book—*The Negative Thoughts Workbook*—is exactly what we all need to put our thoughts in perspective. What I find especially encouraging in reading this excellent workbook is that Dr. Clark integrates a wide range of cognitive behavioral therapy approaches to provide us with the best tools to cope with those annoying, intrusive repetitive negative thoughts.

All of us know what it is like to have these negative thoughts take over. We often feel we have no control over them—we may think that we need to eliminate them completely. Or we may think that we need to "answer" them, engage with them, get "closure" immediately. We cannot leave these thoughts unanswered and unfinished. But the more we try to rid ourselves of the noise in our head, the more those thoughts bounce back to hijack us. You will learn that the harder you try to suppress your thoughts, the stronger they will shout out danger and urgency in your mind. Fortunately, for us, there is a different way—and Dr. Clark leads us on that path.

The nature of repetitive negative thoughts is that we often think we cannot accept uncertainty, we need to know for sure, we need to take control of almost everything, we habitually focus on threat, and we underestimate our ability to solve real problems when they actually do exist. Dr. Clark's workbook reviews the science behind these intrusive thoughts and assumptions and guides us step-by-step to changing these problematic beliefs that fuel our worry and rumination. Dr. Clark helps us realize that certainty is an illusion, that just because we don't control something doesn't mean the world is falling apart, that there is more safety than threat out there, that threat detection is in our head, not in the real world, and that we can actually solve real problems, but we can't solve problems that don't exist.

If any of this rings true for you and you find your tension, anxiety, sleep, or daily functioning interrupted and compromised, then this book is meant for you. As a world-renowned psychologist, Dr. Clark has been working on anxiety for decades, and he brings his knowledge, wisdom, and valuable advice to you in this practical and highly accessible workbook. Think of this as having a world-class personal trainer who shows up and—rather than yell at you to do more on the StairMaster—helps you gently and capably get better control over your mind by giving you the best tools to cope.

Listen to the advice in each chapter, read through the rationale that is based on the state-of-the-art science on worry and rumination, and follow the exercises. You might be surprised to find after working through the many exercises in this excellent workbook that your repetitive negative thoughts are like the background noise from the street. Rather than chasing the fictional ambulance, you may rest content to watch it disappear around the corner. And then you might notice that you can live the life you want to live.

—Robert L. Leahy, PhD
author of *The Worry Cure* and *The Jealousy Cure* and
director of the American Institute for Cognitive Therapy

Introduction

It is easy to feel overwhelmed and confused by the wide range of expert advice and opinions on how to attain emotional healing and wholeness. There are numerous self-help resources at your fingertips, but you were drawn to this workbook for a reason. Maybe you've been feeling anxious, depressed, guilty, or angry for a long time. You're determined to get better, but nothing has helped so far. You're ready for a different approach. It's clear your distress is caused by something bad that happened to you in the past and you can't seem to get over it. Or you've been preoccupied with the possibility of future problems, and you can't stop worrying. In your quest for emotional healing, you've come to realize that the answer is found in:

- Changing how you think

- Taking a more realistic approach to present challenges

- Moving beyond what cannot be changed.

But how do you get there?

This workbook offers a different approach to overcoming emotional distress. It recognizes that anxiety, depression, guilt, and other negative emotions persist because we get stuck in repetitive negative thinking about upsetting personal experiences. This mindset is called *repetitive negative thought* (RNT), and it is the main topic of this workbook. When trapped in uncontrollable negative thinking, we can't help but feel more distressed. It is now recognized that RNT is an important reason why personal distress lingers and that its treatment is important to emotional recovery and well-being (Ehring and Watkins 2008).

Any negative life experience can trigger RNT, such as loss of a valued relationship, school or career failings, family conflict, bad news about your health, financial debt, and threats to health and safety of family members, to name but a few examples. When this happens, we can get caught up in a whirlwind of loss, defeat, threat, or feelings of unfairness. Greater calm and balance will be restored by changing this form of repetitive thinking. Once this happens, you'll be free to deal with your present-day difficulties and take a more accepting approach to what cannot be changed in your life.

Taking the time to work on your RNT can be an important step in your healing journey. I applaud you for the strength of character needed to admit to a personal problem, the determination to get better, and the openness to ask, *What more can I do to overcome my distress?* This attitude will serve you well as you dive into the exercises and worksheets presented in this workbook.

About This Workbook

In the next eight chapters you'll discover how RNT is responsible for the persistence of your emotional distress. Most self-help workbooks focus on a specific condition, like depression or anxiety. *The Negative Thoughts Workbook* is different. It targets a specific symptom that underlies many negative emotions. The first two chapters introduce you to RNT, why it can't be controlled, and how to assess its influence on your emotional well-being. Chapters 3 and 4 provide strategies to overcome two powerful forms of repetitive negative thinking: worry and rumination. These are the most common causes of persistent anxiety and depression. The workbook then moves into territory rarely considered in other self-help resources. Negative emotions, like regret, shame, humiliation, and resentment, are the subjects of chapters 5 through 8. Each chapter deals with a different emotional state. You'll learn whether these emotions are the cause of your distress and how to assess the role of RNT in each emotion. Specific strategies and exercises will help you work through these negative emotions by dealing with your repetitive thinking about past troubling experiences.

Whether your emotional distress is years in the making or the result of a recent disturbing event, working on repetitive negative thoughts is a critical part of recovery from distress. The help you'll find in this workbook is based on years of psychological research that has shown that changing the way we think is an important pathway to emotional health and well-being.

Is This Workbook Right for You?

Emotional distress can take many forms. Its intensity and degree of interference in daily life may differ, but one thing remains common throughout: *the debilitating effects of RNT.* If you've experienced past heartache or fear the future, you'll find the worry and rumination chapters especially helpful. The workbook's assessment tools and strategies are informed by research and relevant to most types of distress, even those that involve a diagnosis and treatment with medication or regular psychotherapy. Whatever the intensity of your distress, you'll find the workbook an important resource in your quest for better emotional health.

The Negative Thoughts Workbook is intended for independent use by individuals with anxiety, depression, guilt, or anger. As you get into the workbook, you may discover its strategies are more effective when used in the context of psychological treatment or counseling sessions. Chapter 1 contains information and assessment tools that will help you decide whether you should be using the workbook with a therapist.

How to Get the Most from the Workbook

Chapters 1 and 2 are mandatory reading because they provide foundational material for the rest of the workbook. The workbook strategies will be less effective if you skip to chapters that seem most relevant to you. Likewise, most people will find chapters 3 and 4 personally relevant because worry and rumination occur in most forms of distress. You can be more selective in your reading of chapters 5 through 8 because they focus on specific types of emotional distress.

As with most workbooks, you will get more from your reading if you take your time and do the exercises in each chapter. You may find some exercises and worksheets more helpful than others, so you'll want to concentrate on them in your daily experience of RNTs. Some exercises have multiple steps, which means they'll require more time and practice than simpler strategies. You'll want to make copies of some of the worksheets, or you can write your responses in the workbook so you have a permanent record. You can download copies of many of the worksheets at the website for this book: http://www.newharbinger.com/45052.

The workbook provides "client" stories and, on occasion, completed worksheets for educational purposes. These are fictitious characters based on the experiences of individuals I've treated with cognitive behavior therapy (CBT) from three decades of work as a clinical psychologist, researcher, and educator.

By reading about this workbook, you've taken an important step toward taking a different approach to your mental health. By this act, you're expressing a desire for change and an openness to new learning. These are wonderful qualities that will help you get much more from your self-help work. I commend you for showing initiative and self-determination, and I hope you will find the time and effort you invest in this workbook of great personal benefit. So let's begin our work together on how you can overcome personal distress by tackling one of its main pillars—*repetitive negative thought.*

CHAPTER 1

•   •   •   •   •

Know Your Mind Traps

Emotional disturbance is often triggered by upsetting or highly stressful life experiences. These events can be so significant that we go through periods of mental anguish that last for months. During that time, our mind tends to repeat the same themes over and over. We can't stop thinking about the negative experience: why it happened, its effects on us, or whether our lives will ever be the same. Or we get caught in endless loops, trying to stop thinking about the experience, assigning blame for what happened, or wondering how to go on living after this terrible development.

Life can go wrong in so many ways. The list of bad experiences is almost endless. Loss of a valued relationship, an injustice committed against you, unfair or dishonest treatment, a career failure, a health threat, financial debt, and a serious mistake or wrongdoing are just a few examples of negative life events. And when bad things happen to good people, this sets the stage for RNT. We can get preoccupied with the event, its causes and consequences, as well as its effect on ourselves and the future. When this happens, RNT becomes the fuel that accelerates our emotional pain and suffering.

This chapter explores RNT and its effects on negative emotion. You'll learn how to determine whether your negative thinking has become excessively repetitive and uncontrollable. The causes and consequences of RNT are explained, and step-by-step instruction and worksheets will help you identify its triggers and emotional impact. Guidelines and recommendations are provided for determining when distress may require professional treatment. We begin with Rhonda, who struggled with worry, one of the most common types of RNT.

Rhonda's Story: Burdened by Worry

Rhonda struggled with anxiety and worry since childhood. Now a working mother approaching forty, life presented her with many opportunities for worry. Whenever she saw her teenage son playing video games rather than doing homework, she worried about his lack of ambition and lack of career aspiration. Her husband, Terry, was overweight and had high blood pressure. Whenever he was winded or complained of not feeling well, she worried that he'd have a heart attack. At work, her manager was cold, critical, and demanding, so she was continually worried about her performance. Even fairly trivial news, like prediction of bad weather, could cause a spiral into worry about getting to work on time the next day. Rhonda seemed able to turn any uncertainty into worry. And when she worried, waves of anxiety swept over her. Sometimes the worry lasted for hours if the concern was especially important. And when that happened, it always involved some future catastrophe: a relentless stream of what-ifs that left her paralyzed with uncertainty. It was an unstoppable force of thought, never leading to a solution or new understanding. For millions like Rhonda, worry is an irresistible "mind trap" that grows stronger the more they struggle against it.

What Are Repetitive Negative Thoughts?

Our mind is constantly thinking. Our survival depends on learning from the past, understanding the present, and anticipating the future. We are planning, problem-solving, and reasoning creatures driven to understand ourselves, our environment, and each other. We are hardwired to produce a stream of thought that ranges from the irrelevant and bizarre to issues of grave personal significance. We tend to think more deeply about the things that matter most and can easily brush off thoughts that matter little to our personal well-being. If our mind functioned perfectly, this is how it would operate. But the mind is not perfect. It can run amuck, causing great personal distress. RNT is one such example.

RNT is found in depression, anxiety, guilt, resentment, shame, and other types of distress. RNT is evident in the examples of Rhonda's worry. It's also apparent in the rumination over unmet goals, such as *Why do I struggle so with depression? What's wrong with me? Why can't I succeed?* or *Why has there been so much loss in my life?* RNT can be found in guilt, such as *I wish I had been less rigid and demanding of my children, I shouldn't have quit university,* or *I should have saved more toward retirement.* RNT might focus on some past shame or embarrassment, like reliving an incident of verbal criticism at an important meeting, thinking back to a disastrous presentation caused by anxiety, or fretting about the time your spouse confronted you about some embarrassing behavior you tried to keep secret. At other times, RNT takes the form of resentment, like thinking back to being unfairly criticized by a close friend, having your hard work taken for granted, or being unjustly punished for some action or decision.

Can you relate to the previous examples of repetitive thought? Or are you left wondering whether RNT is relevant for your distress? To answer this question, a better understanding of RNT is needed. We start with a definition: RNT is *repetitive negative thought that is passive, self-focused, and difficult to control* (Ehring and Watkins 2008). Practically any negative life experience can trigger repeated, uncontrollable negative thought. To determine whether you experience RNT, consider its main features.

- *Repetitive.* RNT is a stubborn form of thought that returns again and again despite your best efforts to think more positively. RNT rarely progresses beyond the same negative themes about yourself or a troubling experience. Rhonda frequently worried about job security. She always came back to the same self-doubts about her level of productivity and the quality of her reports.

- *Negative.* Although any thought can be repetitive, the negative ones are especially potent because they involve some threat to our well-being. We're also more likely to believe our negative thoughts when feeling distressed. Rhonda's worry didn't occur because she was thinking about all the positive things that could happen in the future. Instead, her worry always focused on dark possibilities and their immediate negative consequences.

- *Intrusive.* RNT occurs like a thief in the night. A thought, an image, or a memory may pop into your mind, and before you know it, you're caught in the RNT mind trap. Rhonda could be focused on work, and a thought about her son at school might pop into her mind. This could set off a vicious cycle of worry about his future and lack of ambition, making it difficult to concentrate on work.

- *Unshakable.* It's difficult to switch off negative thinking once it starts. In RNT, negative thinking becomes "sticky," making it difficult to shift attention to positive thoughts. This creates a negativity bias or an imbalance in our thinking style. It was almost impossible for Rhonda to think more positively about her son once worry about his lack of ambition set in. This inability to disengage from negative thinking is especially evident in depression.

- *Uncontrollable.* It can feel like you're losing your mind when caught in the RNT trap. You try hard to think of something else or be more positive, but you quickly return to your negative way of thinking. When worrying about finances, Rhonda kept telling herself, *It will be all right; it'll all work out,* but the reassurance never felt convincing. Her mind would always settle on some financial catastrophe even though she knew it was not rational. At times her worry was so uncontrollable that it caused her to doubt her sanity and level of self-control.

- *Abstract.* When we engage in RNT, we tend to think in an abstract manner. This involves thinking about ourself or a negative experience in a general, hypothetical manner that is disconnected from reality (Watkins 2016). Rhonda experienced RNT about her son's future, but the worrisome thoughts only focused vaguely on blaming herself as a bad parent and imagining her son as a "failed adult." She never thought in specific terms, like how she caused her son's teenage rebelliousness or what it means to be a "failed adult."

- *Passive.* RNT is a passive form of thinking, which means we tend to slip into it without effort or real intention. Rhonda never had to remind herself to worry about her son's school performance. Instead, the worry could hit her out of the blue and then not leave her mind for hours. She might be able to focus on other things, but the worry could linger for a long time in the back of her mind.

Figure 1.1 summarizes the core features of RNT. Now that you understand RNT, complete the next exercise to assess whether your negative thinking takes the form of repetitive negative thought.

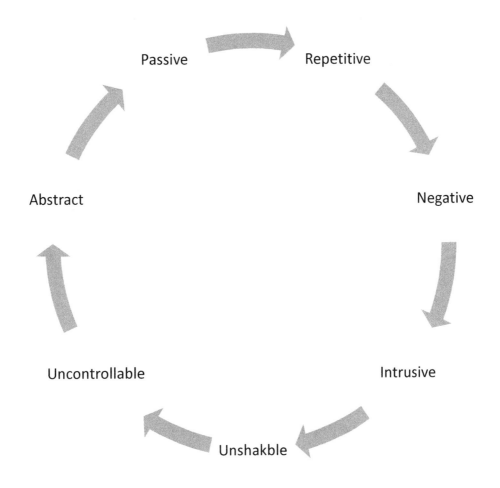

Figure 1.1. Basic Elements of Repetitive Negative Thinking

Exercise: Identify Negative Experiences and Thoughts

Step 1. List up to three negative life experiences that you often think about.

1. _____

2. _____

3. _____

Step 2. Write down any recurring negative thoughts associated with one or more of these experiences. If you have repeated negative thoughts but they are not connected with a negative life event, you can still record these thoughts in the space provided. If you listed additional stressful experiences, write down your repetitive negative thoughts about these experiences as well. You can use additional paper if more space is needed.

1. _____

2. _____

3. _____

Step 3. Look back at the seven characteristics of negative thinking in figure 1.1. Do the thoughts you've listed have these characteristics? Use the checklist to indicate the characteristics that apply to each negative thought.

Negative Thought #1	Negative Thought #2	Negative Thought #3
☐ repetitive	☐ repetitive	☐ repetitive
☐ negative	☐ negative	☐ negative
☐ intrusive	☐ intrusive	☐ intrusive
☐ unshakable	☐ unshakable	☐ unshakable
☐ uncontrollable	☐ uncontrollable	☐ uncontrollable
☐ abstract	☐ abstract	☐ abstract
☐ passive	☐ passive	☐ passive

Is your negative thinking about stressful life experiences consistent with RNT? If you checked most items for your negative thoughts, then your negative thinking may quality as RNT. You'll need to do additional assessment work to be more certain. If you identified other stressful experiences in the first part of this exercise and you'd like to examine them, you can find a version of this exercise online (along with many of the exercises in this book) at http://www.newharbinger.com/45052. You can use the characteristics in step 3 to examine any experiences and thoughts that you suspect may conform to an RNT pattern for you.

The previous exercise is your first glimpse at RNT. After completing the remaining exercises in this chapter, you may want to make changes in the recurring negative thoughts you listed in step 2. If you had difficulty identifying RNT, the next exercise presents a checklist that provides a more comprehensive, in-depth assessment of negative thought and feeling.

The RNT Assessment

You may be still uncertain about the role of RNT in your anxiety, depression, or other negative emotion. Possibly you're so focused on difficulties and emotional distress that you haven't considered how *the way you think affects the way you feel*. Regardless of where you stand on RNT, complete the following checklist for a more detailed assessment of the negative thoughts you listed in the previous exercise.

Exercise: The RNT Checklist

Place a checkmark beside the statements that describe how you experience the negative thoughts listed in the previous exercise.

- ☐ The negative thought about me or an experience returns to my mind over and over.

- ☐ The thought pops into my mind repeatedly throughout the day.

- ☐ Once I start thinking this way, I can't stop myself.

- ☐ The same negative thoughts occur repeatedly without much variation in theme or content.

- ☐ I seem to be irresistibly drawn to the negative thought, even when I don't want to think about it.

☐ I get stuck on the thought and can't shift my attention to something else.

☐ My mind feels like a broken record; I get stuck on the same issues and can't move on.

☐ Despite thinking about this issue over and over, I've made no progress in resolving the problem.

☐ I can't seem to think of me or my experience in a more positive or hopeful manner.

☐ I can't forget about this situation or experience despite my best effort.

☐ I spend a lot of time thinking negatively about me or my experience.

☐ I feel overwhelmed by recurring negative thoughts about me, my life, or my future.

☐ I often wonder what's wrong with me or why a negative experience happened to me.

☐ My repetitive negative thoughts involve a lot of self-blame and criticism.

☐ My mood always gets worse when I am thinking negatively about me or the experience.

There are no established cutoff scores for the RNT Checklist, but if you checked ten or more statements, it's likely your negative thinking fits the criteria for RNT.

These items are based on psychometric studies on recognized RNT measures like the Perseverative Thinking Questionnaire (Ehring et al. 2011), the Repetitive Thinking Questionnaire (McEvoy, Mahoney, and Moulds 2010), and the Ruminative Responses Scale (Treynor, Gonzalez, and Nolen-Hoeksema 2003).

Know the Triggers

RNT doesn't appear out of nowhere. It is often triggered by a comment, a situation, or an intrusive (spontaneous) thought. For Rhonda, her son's flippant comment about boredom with school could trigger intense worry about his future and whether he'll have a "wasted life." Another person sunk into a fresh round of remorseful RNT when he was reminded that he turned down a significant career opportunity. The more RNT you experience, the more easily it becomes triggered by a wider range of situations, reminders, or intrusive thoughts. It is important, then, to know your triggers. Use the following exercise to improve your awareness of RNT triggers.

Exercise: The RNT Triggers Record

Recall times when you experienced RNT. Write down any triggers (situations, comments, memories, or spontaneous thoughts) that may have occurred just before you experienced a repetitive negative thought. Use the following worksheet to record your RNT triggers. You can also download a copy of the RNT Triggers Record at http://www.newharbinger.com/45052.

Day	Triggers: Situation, Context	Triggers: Spontaneous (Intrusive) Thought, Feeling	Triggers: Intrusive Memory
(Rhonda's examples)	*Manager had serious look on his face while reading my report.* *Coworker tells about her daughter's scholarship.* *Over lunch, a friend talks about her neighbor having a heart attack.*	*Spontaneous thought about son not paying attention in class.* *Sudden thought of family doctor's warning to husband at his last visit.*	*Intrusive image of driving home on snowy roads.*

Review your worksheet and see what you can learn about the kinds of situations, thoughts, memories, or feelings that triggered your RNT. Ask yourself:

- Do I notice any patterns?

- Do I react more to some situations than others?

- Am I particularly sensitive to certain comments from other people?

- Is my repetitive negative thinking often triggered by an unwanted intrusive thought?

Write down your impressions here, continuing on a separate piece of paper or in a journal if you run out of space. If you can't recall RNT experiences, keep track of your recurring negative thoughts over the next three days and record the triggers on the worksheet.

_____

_____

_____

_____

_____

_____

Having better awareness of your trigger sensitivities is a necessary step in changing how you deal with RNT and its distress. You'll want to focus the RNT strategies presented in subsequent chapters on your triggers. Rather than continue with avoidance, you'll want to do more work on changing how you react to your RNT triggers.

Trapped in Your Head: The Consequences of RNT

Once triggered, RNT has a negative effect on how we think, feel, and behave. In figure 1.2 these effects are illustrated as a vicious cycle in which the effects build on each other, causing greater interference in daily living.

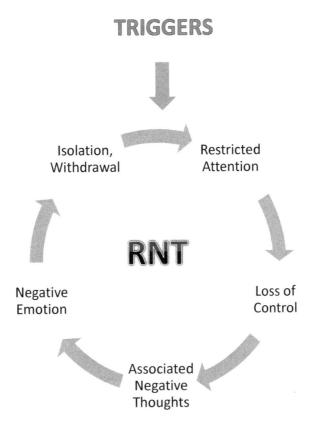

Figure 1.2. The Negative Effects of RNT

The first negative effect of RNT is the narrowing of attention onto certain negative thought content. When Rhonda worried about her son, she could only think of him as a young man who failed to live up to his potential. She had difficulty thinking of him in any other way. She'd get locked into this negative theme, and her mind seemed incapable of considering other alternatives.

When trapped in the RNT experience, we feel a loss of mental control. We know our biased negative thinking is self-defeating, but we're powerless to free ourselves from the mental gridlock. We want to think more positively, but the harder we try, the more compelling the negative thoughts are. This sense of uncontrollability can cause considerable insecurity and self-doubt, strengthening unhelpful beliefs that we're weak, a failure, defeated, or undeserving. Anxious thoughts of personal threat and danger become overpowering, and thoughts of a hopeless future appear self-evident.

RNT has its greatest effect on feelings and behavior. When caught in RNT, people become more anxious, depressed, frustrated, irritable, guilty, and even angry. They may prefer solitude and avoid socializing with friends and family. Rhonda most often refused the invitations of close friends, preferring instead to spend evenings and weekends at home alone or with her family. Socializing was becoming harder and less enjoyable as she spent more and more time in her own head. This provided greater opportunity to engage in other forms of negative thought, like biased self-evaluation, post-event processing, and defensive pessimism. To fully understand the personal impact of RNT, take a few minutes to complete the next exercise.

Exercise: The RNT Consequences Scale

Below is a scale with several statements that describe ways that RNT can negatively impact your daily living and life satisfaction. Use the three-point rating scale to indicate the relevance of each statement for your experience of RNT.

Statements	Not Relevant	Somewhat Relevant	Very Relevant
1. Practically anything can cause me to slip into episodes of repetitive negative thinking.	0	1	2
2. My negative thinking tends to focus on one or two themes, and so it is highly repetitive.	0	1	2
3. I get stuck in negative thinking and can't see things differently.	0	1	2
4. I become overwhelmed with negative thinking and can't seem to control it.	0	1	2
5. Once it starts, I can't seem to stop thinking negatively.	0	1	2
6. I often feel like I am losing control over my mind.	0	1	2
7. When I am stuck in negative thinking, I become more self-critical.	0	1	2
8. I'm concerned about my mental health or ability to be happy when experiencing RNT.	0	1	2
9. I think I'm being punished in some way by my relentless negative thinking.	0	1	2
10. I feel guilty for getting stuck in negative thought.	0	1	2
11. When I experience RNT, I feel more and more depressed.	0	1	2
12. I feel anxious or frustrated when I can't stop the repetitive negative thoughts.	0	1	2
13. I prefer to be alone and do nothing when caught in cycles of negative thinking.	0	1	2
14. I spend more time in bed or just resting when I have an episode of RNT.	0	1	2
15. I avoid social contact when experiencing RNT.	0	1	2

RNT might be having a significant negative impact on your emotional well-being if you circled 1 or 2 on ten or more statements. The scale was constructed for this workbook, so there is no independent research to determine its validity or accuracy. It should be used as a rough guide to indicate whether RNT may be a significant factor in your emotional disturbance.

As you continue to work on your RNT in subsequent chapters, you'll want to refer to these assessment worksheets so you can determine how much you've reduced the negative effects of RNT. Possibly you've completed the assessment exercises, and it's clear that RNT is a major issue in your life. Now perhaps you are wondering whether to continue with the workbook on your own or whether you should be working with a mental health therapist (if you're not already engaged in therapy). The next section provides some guidance on this question.

When to Seek Professional Help

The Negative Thoughts Workbook is a self-help resource written for the general public. However, many people find that self-help alone is not enough. They realize the help of a qualified mental health professional may lead to deeper and more enduring change. If you are seeing a therapist for emotional distress, the workbook exercises can be included in your therapy, especially if you are receiving CBT. You should inform your therapist of any self-help material you are reading, which includes this workbook. If you are not receiving mental health treatment, consult with a qualified mental health professional when the emotional distress is intense, is persistent, causes significant interference in daily functioning, or is associated with a traumatic experience. In addition, you should seek professional help if you experience a fairly sudden reduction in emotional functioning characterized by a significant alteration in personality. The advice of family members and close friends can be helpful because they are often more aware of distinct changes in our emotional state and functioning. The following checklist provides a few indicators you can use to determine when to seek a mental health consultation.

Exercise: The Emotional Distress Checklist

Read the following statements and place a checkmark in the "Yes" column if the statement describes how you've been thinking, feeling, or behaving in the last month or more.

Statements	Yes	No
1. I experience very intense bouts of depression, anxiety, anger, or other negative emotions.		
2. When I get depressed or otherwise upset, the depression can last for days or even weeks at a time.		
3. I have little control over my distress when it occurs.		
4. When I am upset, it greatly interferes with my daily functioning.		
5. I often have suicidal or self-harming thoughts.		
6. I have poor sleep most nights.		
7. When upset, I tend to isolate myself and withdraw from others.		
8. I have problems controlling my anger and can be quite hurtful toward others.		
9. When upset, anxious, or depressed, I rely on procrastination and avoidance to deal with life's demands.		
10. When feeling anxious or depressed, I tend to use alcohol or other substances to ease the emotional pain.		
11. I haven't been able to experience positive emotions, like joy, peace, or contentment, for weeks.		
12. My emotions fluctuate from one extreme to the other.		
13. I often get into conflict or arguments with friends, coworkers, or acquaintances.		
14. When emotionally upset, frustrated, or angry, I can become verbally or physically aggressive.		
15. I have thoughts and ideas that other people find bizarre or even disturbing.		
16. I am having trouble doing even the routine activities of daily living.		
17. I have noticed a significant decline in my memory and concentration.		

If you checked several of these statements, you should consider speaking to your family physician or a mental health professional about your emotional state. This list does not include all the indicators that health professionals use to determine the presence of a mental disorder.

Only a thorough diagnostic assessment from a qualified mental health professional can determine whether your distress meets the criteria of a psychiatric or psychological disorder. The Emotional Distress Checklist is a screening instrument. If you checked several statements, you might find this workbook more effective if you used it with the guidance and supervision of a mental health therapist.

Wrap-Up

In this chapter you learned:

- Negative emotional states, like depression, anxiety, guilt, anger, and shame, often persist because people get stuck in a negative mindset.

- There is a special type of mental distress, called repetitive negative thought (RNT), that traps people into a negative perspective about themselves, their life circumstances, and the future.

- RNT is a passive, intrusive, uncontrollable, and abstract form of thought that is most commonly experienced as anxious worry or depressive rumination.

- RNT contributes to personal distress by narrowing our attention, intensifying a sense of lost control, magnifying negative thoughts and feelings, and promoting social withdrawal and isolation.

- Knowing whether your negative thinking qualifies as RNT and determining its effect on you is the first step in freeing yourself from this mental gridlock.

- Everyone has experienced personal distress at some point in their life. Knowing the limits of self-recovery from depression, anxiety, and other negative emotions is important for getting the most from this workbook.

What's Next?

Now that you've gained a greater understanding of your repetitive negative thoughts and recurring distress, it is time to consider a second major contributor: loss of self-control. For decades, psychologists have recognized a close relationship between the frequency and intensity of negative thoughts and a feeling of controllability. When unwanted thoughts are frequent and distressing, we feel a loss of self-control. Just when we are in most need of control, it seems to vanish. This creates a dilemma, which can be called "the mental control paradox." We'll talk about this in chapter 2.

CHAPTER 2

. . . . .

Manage the Control Paradox

Self-control is the cornerstone of emotional health and well-being. We all strive to improve self-control over our feelings and behavior. At the same time, many of our regrets involve times when we lost control, especially in front of others. We admire people who can turn off worry when faced with uncertainty or can move beyond past failures and mistakes without slipping into discouragement, guilt, or defeat. There is plenty of research to support this sentiment. High self-control is an important ingredient for emotional health, long-term success, and life satisfaction.

The importance of self-control extends to our mind. Our brain is continually generating thousands of thoughts, images, perceptions, and memories. We must direct our attention to the *thoughts* that are important and ignore the ones that don't matter. This requires a considerable amount of mental self-control. Our mind's ability to distinguish between important and unimportant thoughts is rooted in the part of the brain called the prefrontal cortex. Unfortunately, mental self-control is not perfect, so we often pay too much attention to irrelevant thoughts, or we get stuck on unhelpful, even toxic, ways of thinking. This is what happens in RNT.

In the last chapter you were introduced to Rhonda, who struggled with generalized anxiety and worry. One of her worries concerned finances and whether she was saving enough for retirement. Her excessive worry is a prime example of failed mental control. She'd tell herself, *Don't worry; retirement is a long way off.* But this advice never helped. No matter how hard she tried, the worry continued. It's as if she was running into a mental brick wall! The more she tried to control the worry, the less she felt in control. Rhonda was living out the *mental control paradox.*

If you've ever competed, you know that your performance can get worse if you try too hard. "Trying too hard" is the main theme of this chapter. It's central to the mental control paradox. You'll learn that letting go of control is the best way to gain control over RNT. As well, you'll discover whether you're relying too much on ineffective rather than more effective thought-control strategies. Exercises and worksheets will help you highlight problems with your efforts to control the RNT that contributes to your emotional distress.

White Bears and the Paradox of Mental Control

Let's begin with white bears! One of our most basic mental abilities is the capacity to direct our attention and concentration to task-relevant thoughts and not get distracted by task-irrelevant thinking. As an example, I need enough mental control to focus on ideas that are relevant to writing this paragraph and to ignore intrusive thoughts like, *What will I have for lunch?* But self-control is not limitless, and it can fail us at times when we need it most. Have you noticed this about control over your thinking? On some occasions, you have great powers of concentration, but then at other times, your mental control is weak and you are easily distracted.

Psychologists have learned a great deal about the mysteries of mental control. One of the most important questions is, *How much control do we have over unwanted emotional thoughts?* Is it possible to willfully banish recurrent, unwanted thoughts from our mind? Let's begin by considering the limits of mental control and what this means for the work you'll doing in this workbook.

Much of our knowledge about the limits of mental control comes from an ingenious experiment developed by the late Harvard psychologist Daniel Wegner (1994). He showed that asking people to *not* think about a white bear for two minutes caused an *increase* in white bear thoughts in a subsequent two-minute period. Numerous "white bear" studies have been performed since that original experiment. These studies indicate that our ability to *not think* (suppress) unwanted thoughts is limited, and often such efforts eventually lead to more unwanted thoughts. But don't take my word for it. Try it yourself with the following exercise.

Exercise: The White Bear Experiment

There are two parts to the experiment. The first, called "thought retention," tests how well you can keep your attention focused on a single thought. Close your eyes and think about a white bear. You should try as hard as you can to keep your mind focused on the white bear. If other thoughts pop into your mind, simply note the interruption with a tally mark on a blank sheet of paper, and then gently return your attention to the white bear. After two minutes, open your eyes and count the number of interruptions you experienced while trying to think about a white bear. Record the number of thought interruptions and rate your experience using the three-point scale below.

Thought Retention

1. Number of thought interruptions: _____

2. Success in staying focused: 0 = not at all successful, 1 = slightly successful, 2 = very successful

3. How much effort was needed to *stay focused* on the white bear: 0 = no effort, 1 = slight effort, 2 = great deal of effort

The second part of the experiment is called "thought dismissal." Once again, close your eyes, and for the next two minutes, try not to think about a white bear. You should try as hard as you can to suppress or prevent any thought of a white bear from entering your mind. If the white bear thought pops into your mind, make a tally mark on the sheet of paper, and then gently turn your attention to other thoughts. Use the following scales to record your experience of trying not to think of a white bear.

Thought Dismissal

1. Number of times the white bear thought intruded: _____

2. Success in suppressing the white bear thought: 0 = not at all successful, 1 = slightly successful, 2 = very successful

3. How much effort was needed to *not think* about the white bear: 0 = no effort, 1 = slight effort, 2 = great deal of effort

Did you find it much harder to suppress the white bear thought (dismissal) than to keep it in your mind (retention)? What surprised you most, the effort needed to keep your attention focused on a single thought or the effort needed to suppress an unwanted thought? Most people find it harder to suppress the white bear thought and are often surprised at their weak suppression ability.

Was the exercise a good reminder that our mental control is limited? In a small way, you also experienced the negative effects of trying not to think about something. Imagine how much harder suppression would be if the thought was important to you, like a profound regret, and you were trying to "not think" of it for hours or days on end. Trying *not to think* about something that is personally significant may cause more negative effects than trying to suppress an insignificant thought like a white bear. With something important, you'd become more preoccupied with the unwelcomed intrusion. You'd find it harder to shift your attention to something else because you'd be telling yourself, *I've got to stop thinking so negatively.* Your repeated failure to control the thought would cause greater frustration, anxiety, guilt, or discouragement. In the end, your emotional distress would intensify as the thought kept returning again and again. This is what we mean by the mental control paradox as illustrated in figure 2.1.

 Greater Mental Effort = Poorer Mental Control

Figure 2.1. The Mental Control Paradox

Rhonda tried hard not to worry about her husband's health. Whenever it started, she tried to squelch the worry by reassuring herself that everything will be fine. She recited health statistics on the probability of death for middle-aged American men with cardiac risk factors. But this didn't help. The more she tried to suppress the worry, the more it took hold of her mind. It seemed like the worry was unbeatable. Unbeknownst to Rhonda, she was falling prey to the mental control paradox.

Letting Go of Control

Has the white bear exercise left you feeling discouraged about the prospects of gaining control over your distressing thoughts? You've known for some time that it's impossible to simply stop all control effort and ignore what's in your mind. Telling yourself, *Don't pay any attention to it; just think about something else, and I'll be fine,* doesn't work. There are several reasons why.

- We naturally pay more attention to emotional thoughts.

- Trying to *not think* takes a great deal of mental effort.

- Repetitive negative thoughts deal with concerns that matter to us.

- RNTs grab our attention more easily than other types of thought.

- RNTs are usually consistent with how we feel at the moment, so they have greater staying power in the mind.

If our repetitive distressing thoughts are so sticky that we can't ignore them, a new approach to letting go is needed. This begins with being convinced that trying harder to ignore, suppress, or distract yourself doesn't work for RNTs. Maybe you were surprised by the white bear results, but you're still thinking your problem is poor self-control. If so, try doing the next exercise, which more directly tests the effects of mental control effort on unwanted, distressing thoughts. Called the Alternate-Days Experiment, it's based on a similar exercise described in *The Anxious Thoughts Workbook* (Clark 2018, 96–97).

Exercise: The Alternate-Days Experiment

Write down your main repetitive negative thought in the space provided. This could be one of the RNTs you listed in the first exercise in chapter 1.

_____

_____

Select two weekdays to do the alternate-days experiment. One day will be low mental control, and the next, high mental control. During the low-control day, devote as little attention as possible to intentionally controlling the RNT when it pops into your mind. Allow yourself to think or feel whatever comes into your mind without consciously trying to control what you are thinking or feeling. That is, let go of your mental-control effort over the RNT. On the high-control day, pay close attention to the RNT whenever it pops into your mind, and do your best to get the thought out of your head.

At the end of each day, briefly describe your experience with giving up on controlling the thought versus trying hard *not to think* of the RNT. Your description should be detailed enough so you can answer the questions that follow and list the advantages of lesser versus greater mental control.

Observation About Low-Control Day	Observation About High-Control Day

Based on your observations, answer the following questions about your experience with letting go of control versus high mental-control effort.

- Did you have fewer problems with the RNT and less distress when engaged in low control compared to the high-effort control day, or did you find little difference between the two conditions?

  _____

  _____

- Were you more frustrated or stressed when trying hard to control the RNT? Were you less upset with yourself when you let go of control?

  _____

  _____

- Was the greater effort at controlling the repetitive negative thought worth it? List the advantages of low-control versus high-control effort.

Advantages of Low-Control Effort	Advantages of High-Control Effort

What's your conclusion about trying hard to ignore, suppress, or prevent repetitive negative thinking? Did you have less anxiety, depression, anger, or guilt with low control? Or was there little difference in your thoughts and feelings on both days? If you've come to either conclusion, then you're ready to let go of control. You've discovered that trying hard to push the unwanted thought from your mind is simply not worth it.

Maybe you still have some doubts about letting go of mental control, or possibly you found it too difficult to let your mind wander on the low-control day. Learning to let go of control is an important skill that will be included in many of the strategies you'll learn about in subsequent chapters.

Troubleshoot Your Control Strategies

Knowing your limits is the first step in letting go of control. The second step requires a closer analysis of the actual control strategies used to in response to your RNTs.

We know that some mental control responses are more helpful than others (Wegner 2011). Unfortunately, we're more likely to use unhelpful control strategies with personally significant distressing thoughts (Levine and Warman 2016). So we may be more inclined to use less effective mental control strategies when experiencing RNT.

It's hard to do nothing when a distressing thought repeatedly pops into our mind. We assume the RNT must be significant because of its recurrence. So we assign it greater attentional priority, which means we have to engage in some form of mental control if we want to shift our attention away from the unwanted thought.

Our mental control responses happen in a split second. This means you'll be into a control response before you know it. But with training and effort, you can increase your awareness of these responses because they likely happen many times throughout the day. Table 2.1 presents a list of common mental control responses. They are categorized as relatively effective or ineffective in their ability to shift attention away from unwanted negative thinking (Wegner 2011; Wells and Davies 1994).

Table 2.1 *Common Mental Control Responses*

Effective Strategies	Ineffective Strategies
Replace with another thought.	Try to reason with yourself.
Engage in an activity to distract yourself.	Criticize yourself for thinking this way.
Just accept the thought; let it "float" through your mind without engaging the repetitive thought.	Seek reassurance from others.
Try to view the negative thought in a more positive, helpful manner.	Tell yourself to stop thinking this way.
Try to relax, meditate, or breathe slowly.	Analyze the meaning to determine why you are thinking like this.
Find humor in how you are thinking.	Look for evidence that refutes the RNT.
	Repeat a phrase or an action (for example, checking something) that counters (neutralizes) the thought or reduces distress.
	Actively suppress thinking about the RNT.
	Pray or focus on a comforting phrase or idea.
	Try to reassure yourself that everything will be fine.
	Perform a compulsive ritual.
	Avoid situations, objects, or people that might trigger the RNT.

Read through table 2.1 slowly, taking time to think about your own way of responding to negative thinking. Do you have certain go-to strategies? Are they from the effective or ineffective category? If you are not using the more effective control responses, this could explain why it feels like you've lost control of RNT. Most people are so focused on how bad they feel that they never consider how their response to the negative thoughts might contribute to the distress.

Adopt Effective Mental Control

Some mental control strategies are effective but are challenging to master. Cognitive restructuring, mindfulness, and positive self-affirmation are effective strategies used in psychological treatments for anxiety and depression. Cognitive restructuring and mindfulness are evidence-based interventions, but they are hard to learn without instruction from a mental health professional. Other control strategies, like avoidance, reassurance seeking, and self-criticism, should not be used because they make negative thinking worse.

The effectiveness of the seven control strategies listed in the first column in table 2.1 are relatively more helpful in dealing with RNT than other strategies. Also, you can expect that effectiveness of any control strategy to vary depending on your level of distress and the circumstances that trigger the RNT. This is illustrated by the "effectiveness arrow" depicted in figure 2.2.

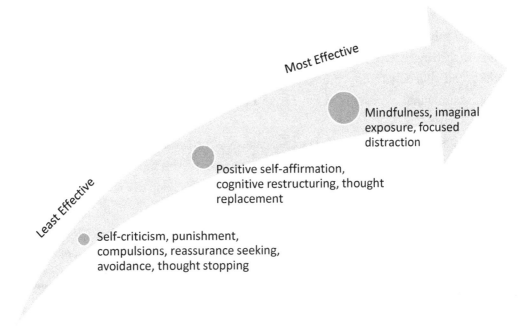

Figure 2.2. The Mental Control Effectiveness Arrow

The mental control strategies at the bottom end of the arrow directly confront a negative thought and are used to banish the thought from conscious awareness. If there is any effectiveness to these strategies, it's short-lived. The RNT eventually returns with even greater intensity.

When worried about finances or her husband's safety, Rhonda tried to reassure herself that everything will be all right, or she would berate herself as a worrywart. She was never comforted by the self-reassurance, and the *self-criticism* just made her feel worse. In the end, the vicious cycle of worry continued without interruption.

The strategies listed in the middle section of the arrow are moderately effective. Bringing to mind your positive qualities and attributes (*self-affirmation*), questioning the truthfulness of the RNT (*cognitive restructuring*), and *replacing the recurring negative thought* with a positive or neutral thought are somewhat effective in controlling negative thoughts and feelings. These strategies also require direct engagement with the RNT, and so you never entirely let go of control with these strategies.

The most effective mental control strategies take a more passive, detached approach to negative thinking and so offer the best hope for dealing with RNT. *Mindfulness* involves taking a more distant, observer perspective in which the negative thought is allowed "to sit in one's mind" without response or judgment. With *imaginal exposure*, the individual intentionally brings the RNT to mind for a specific period of time. *Focused distraction* takes a more systematic approach to shifting attention from the RNT to a highly engaging mental or behavioral activity. Rhonda found that scheduling time each evening to generate and fully reflect on the feared catastrophe (imaginal exposure) at the center of her worry paradoxically led to a reduction in anxiety and worry.

Table 2.2 provides the definitions and examples of the mental control strategies in the effectiveness arrow, with the more therapeutic strategies at the top and the least therapeutic at the bottom. As you read the definitions and examples, consider whether you use any of these strategies when you feel distressed. Don't be too concerned if you're finding it hard to see how these strategies apply to your emotional distress. This is your first introduction to these concepts. The subsequent chapters that deal with specific types of RNT will draw heavily on this table and explain how to apply these mental control strategies more effectively in the management of your RNT.

Table 2.2. *Therapeutic and Nontherapeutic Mental Control Strategies*

Strategy	Explanation	Example
Mindfulness	Passively observing the unwanted repetitive thought, accepting it, and letting the thought sit in your mind without evaluation or effortful control.	Whenever a serious past mistake is remembered, the memory of the incident is allowed to float in and out of conscious awareness without judgment or effort to control it.
Focused distraction	Shifting attention to a single highly engaging idea, memory, or activity that more fully captures information processing resources.	When getting stuck in thinking about a bad experience, a person switches her attention to redesigning her garden, given her deep passion for this activity.
Positive self-affirmation	Thinking deeply about your positive qualities and attributes in a compassionate manner that emphasizes your moral competence and goodness.	When having repeated thoughts of guilt for past wrongdoing, a person brings to mind specific examples of being a loving parent, a loyal and caring friend, a competent and dependable worker, and the like.
Cognitive restructuring	Systematically gathering evidence that questions the accuracy of an RNT and then discovering a more realistic way of thinking that guides subsequent coping responses.	When thinking over and over, *Why have I experienced more loss than others?* the individual gathers evidence that supports versus refutes this perspective, and then generates a more realistic alternative, such as, *Some people experience more loss than others even when they don't bring it on themselves.*

Strategy	Explanation	Example
Thought replacement	Shifting attention from the RNT to a more positive or neutral thought.	When the anxious thought, *Is she cheating on me?* repeatedly comes to mind, the individual tries to think about the last sports game he watched.
Reassurance seeking	Seeking confirmation from other people or external sources that everything will be fine, and the distress associated with the RNT will subside.	When experiencing recurrent anxious thoughts about an unexpected physical ache or pain, the individual searches the internet for reassuring information that the symptom is benign, and her health is fine.
Avoidance	Trying to refrain or escape from situations, thoughts, or feelings that might trigger RNT.	The individual avoids people, situations, or conversation that might trigger a fresh round of worry about her job security or an impending performance review.
Thought stopping	Making explicit self-verbalizations like "stop thinking this way!"	Whenever memory of a humiliating experience pops into his mind, the individual feels intense frustration and yells, "STOP!" under his breath.
Compulsions	Performing specific mental or behavioral rituals to reduce distress or cancel out the feared consequences of an RNT.	The individual repeats a specific religious phrase that creates a sense of inner cleanliness whenever recurrent thoughts of moral violation or impurity enters her mind.
Self-criticism or punishment	Generating critical or derogatory self-evaluations because of RNT and its uncontrollability.	The individual verbalizes statements to himself like, "Don't be so stupid," "I must be going crazy," "I'm weak and pathetic."

Are you familiar with any of the "therapeutic" mental control strategies described in table 2.2? Possibly you were introduced to these strategies by a therapist, but you've drifted away from using them. Can you recall a time when you found the strategies helpful in dealing with distressing thoughts and feelings? Or the strategies may be completely unfamiliar to you. Maybe the less-effective strategies, like reassurance seeking, avoidance, and self-criticism, seem more familiar because you've been falling back on them when feeling distressed. Whatever the case, you'll learn in subsequent chapters how to modify these strategies to reduce various types of RNT.

The final exercise in this chapter provides the opportunity to take a closer look at how you respond to negative thoughts that are, at most, mildly distressing. You're probably well aware of using unhelpful mental control strategies. It may be less obvious that you're using effective mental control with less distressing negative thoughts. This next exercise focuses on this issue and whether you may discover an effective control strategy you are already using.

Exercise: Discover Your Best Strategy

Select a typical weekday to be more aware of any negative thoughts that pop into your mind. Be especially mindful of negative thoughts *not* related to your RNT. On these occasions you are thinking negatively, but it's only slightly distressing and does not interfere with daily functioning. You can take notes (in writing or in voice memos on your phone) when the thought is happening or just make a mental note of what's happening in your mind. At the end of the day, jot down the thoughts and how you coped with them in the space provided:

1. Negative thought: _____

   My response: _____

2. Negative thought:_____

   My response: _____

3. Negative thought:_____

   My response: _____

4. Negative thought:_____

   My response: _____

5. Negative thought:_____

    My response: _____

Next, rate how often you used each of the following relatively effective control strategies in response to your *nondistressing negative thinking*, where 0 is never, 1 is some of the time, and 2 is much of the time.

Mindfulness or meditation _____

Focused distraction _____

Positive self-affirmation _____

Cognitive restructuring _____

Thought replacement _____

Did you discover that you used some of the control strategies more than the others? If so, these strategies may feel most comfortable to you. You'll want to focus on improving these strategies so they're more effective in controlling RNT. You may want to complete this exercise over multiple days. You can print copies of this exercise at the website for this book: http://www.newharbinger.com/45052.

In subsequent chapters, you can be more strategic in your control responses by starting with strategies you use when mildly distressed. You'll learn how to improve the effectiveness of these natural strategies by modifying their content so they address the unique characteristics of each type of RNT.

Some strategies may feel more acceptable to you than others because you're already using them successfully with other types of negative thinking. They are probably a better fit with your personality and natural abilities. Cognitive restructuring, for example, is often preferred by people who are more analytic, whereas more intuitive people might prefer a mindfulness or meditation approach. As you continue with the workbook, spend more time on the control strategies that are a better fit for you. Ultimately, the goal is learning to respond differently to your RNT so you get to the point of letting go of control.

Wrap-Up

In this chapter you learned:

- Our ability to control unwanted thoughts is limited.

- There is a paradox to mental control: the greater the effort, the less you succeed.

- The best strategy for RNT is letting go of control. This involves reducing mental control effort and developing greater tolerance for the unwanted thoughts.

- Disengagement control strategies are more effective for RNT than direct confrontation and avoidance.

- You can work on strengthening thought control strategies that feel more natural and are effective in reducing mildly distressing negative thoughts.

What's Next?

Congratulations on working through these initial chapters. No one likes to read theory and background, but the knowledge you've gained in these chapters will provide a foundation for what comes next. The therapeutic strategies presented for specific problems like worry, rumination, regret, and the like will make more sense because of what you've read in these chapters. As you continue with the workbook, you'll want to come back to these chapters to refresh your understanding of RNT and its control. So let's get started on applying what you've learned to specific emotional problems. The next chapter delves into worry, the most common form of RNT.

CHAPTER 3

Kick the Worry Habit

Worrying seems as natural as breathing. How can it be any different? Life can be difficult and the future uncertain, so we worry that much bigger problems are on the horizon. Excessive worry is a basic feature of anxiety, especially *generalized anxiety disorder* (GAD). So, if you've ever felt apprehensive or had to confront a personally threatening situation, there's a good chance you worried.

Not everyone worries the same way. When worry is chronic, it may occur much of the day, even about minor matters, and can be impossible to control. When this happens, worry has become a serious health problem. Most of us understand worry about serious problems, like a life-threatening illness, loss of a valued relationship, or career failure. But chronic worriers can fret about fairly mundane responsibilities, like getting to an appointment on time, dealing with traffic, doing household chores, or preparing a meal. Despite the worrier's efforts to be rational and reassure themselves that everything will be fine, the worry lingers and with it a feeling of dread. We'll call this *maladaptive worry*, and it meets all the criteria of RNT discussed in chapter 1.

Maladaptive worry doesn't always make sense. You'd expect worry to be greatest in people experiencing a lot of life difficulties. This isn't the case. Older adults worry less than younger adults, despite facing deteriorating health, fixed incomes, and death of loved ones (Gonçalves and Byrne 2013), and excessive worry is more common in high-income countries (Rusico et al. 2017). So, having a relatively easy and stress-free life is no guarantee against worry. But this is good news because having a difficult life doesn't mean you have to worry. No matter what life throws your way, someone else has it worse, and they're not paralyzed with worry.

Worry is such a natural response that we must start by being clear on what is meant by excessive, maladaptive worry. It's this type of worry that qualifies as RNT. In this chapter, you'll find guidelines and assessment tools to help you determine if you experience RNT worry. You'll discover the distinction between realistic, productive worry and the irrational, maladaptive type. If your worry is associated with significant life problems, you'll learn how to use problem solving to ease your worry. Most chronic worry focuses on imaginative, improbable outcomes, so decatastrophizing and systematic worry exposure are the best strategies for addressing this worry type. But before we continue, consider Liam's struggle with debilitating worry.

Liam's Story: Worried Sick

Liam, in his fourth year of a very demanding premedical school program, struggled with anxiety and worry. The oldest son in a high-achieving, middle-class family, Liam felt the pressure of high expectations from an early age. As a child, Liam developed a passion for medicine, no doubt sensing his self-worth depended on having a medical career. He knew getting accepted into medical school was tough because of the competition and high admissions standards. Liam had lots of ability, but his grades had to be outstanding, and his resume had to show he was talented, caring, and a well-rounded person. He studied long and hard to get the best grades possible and took the most difficult courses to ensure he had the strongest possible medical school application. But Liam was tortured with self-doubt, insecurity, and worry.

Intense worry of not doing well enough occurred days before every test, exam, and assignment. He never felt like he knew the material well enough, so he was driven to study much longer than needed. He was not sleeping well, which also caused worry because he feared its effect on his academic performance. He worried he was not as intelligent as his peers and that his professors might think he didn't have the ability for medicine. He constantly sought his mother's reassurance that he'd get accepted into medical school. The worry of medical school was constantly on his mind, and it was now affecting his health. He was having severe abdominal pain and headaches, which doctors attributed to stress and anxiety. His family doctor warned Liam to get ahold of his anxiety or he'd have to take a term off school. This caused further worry because now Liam was worried about being worried. Liam's worry was out of control and threatening his most cherished dreams. Does Liam's preoccupation with an uncertain future sound familiar? Are you also experiencing "runaway worry"?

The Irresistible Urge to Worry

Worry is about life and its uncertainties. It's triggered by our most cherished life concerns, goals, and responsibilities. We worry about changes or difficulties in family and peer relationships, health and safety of self or significant others, work or school, finances, world events and, in some cases, minor issues, like house repairs, being on time for appointments, or doing errands. Most often worry is about negative life events, but even positive changes, like the birth of a child or starting a new job, can trigger a fresh round of worry.

If you've struggled with worry most of your life, you might be convinced there's nothing you can do about it. You might believe worry runs in your family, so you're destined to be a worrywart. Life is complicated and uncertain, so there's lots to worry about. But worry is not a birthright. Often, we learn to worry at an early age and then spend the remaining years reinforcing the habit. Liam blamed his worry on the stress and demands of his courses. It was the circumstances of his life that caused worry. But the reality is that Liam worried excessively about many things, like his health and relationships. Worry was becoming his go-to response whenever he thought about the future.

Getting a handle on worry begins with understanding its irresistible nature. Consider the following definition:

> Worry is a persistent, repetitive, and uncontrollable chain of thinking that mainly focuses on the uncertainty of some future negative or threatening outcome in which the person rehearses various problem-solving solutions but fails to reduce the heightened sense of uncertainty about the possible threat (Clark and Beck 2012, 235).

Let's unpack the definition. There are six features of worry that can make it irresistible:

- *Uncertainty.* Worry is always about some future calamity or undesired outcome. You can think of worry as the "what-if disease." *What if I don't get the promotion? What if the medical test result comes back positive? What if I never find true love?* When caught up in the world of what-ifs, we're questioning a future that is beyond our control. We can't know the future. We can make predictions, but we can't guarantee what the future holds. So, everyone is forced to live with uncertainty, but some people find this more difficult than others (Dugus and Robichaud 2007). This places them at higher risk for chronic worry.

- *Uncontrollability.* Excessive worry is unstoppable even though you realize it is futile and upsetting. Chronic worriers tell themselves to "stop worrying," or they hear this from others, but they can't help it. Liam couldn't stop his worry even though he knew it was pointless and probably harming his academic performance.

- *Threat focus.* People who worry tend to be pessimists. Their mind is programmed to notice things that confirm a belief in a dangerous, threatening, and unjust world. It's harder for the worried person to see safety and security or to think of the future in a positive manner because this is inconsistent with their worldview. When Liam thought of medical school, he could only think about getting rejection letters and the feeling of shame and defeat that would bring.

- *Ineffective control.* Worriers are known to use ineffective strategies when caught in a worry cycle. Reassurance seeking, avoidance, self-criticism, and reasoning are often the go-to responses, but these are quite ineffective strategies for RNT (as discussed in chapter 2).

- *Positive beliefs.* Given the negative effects of worry, it's interesting that chronic worriers often believe that worry is helpful. We're more likely to worry if we believe (a) worry helps with problem solving, (b) it increases motivation, (c) it helps lessen the impact of a negative event, or (d) it's a sign of strong character (Wells 2009). Even though Liam could feel "sick with worry," he believed that worry scared him into being better prepared for his exams.

- *Failed problem solving.* Chronic worriers have pretty good problem-solving skills. Where they go wrong is (a) exaggerating the degree of threat in a situation, (b) having low confidence in their problem-solving ability, and (c) being pessimistic about their solutions (Dugas and Robichaud 2007). They may require a higher level of certainty with their decisions, so they end up flipping from one possible course of action to another. Does this happen with your worry? Do you fret, scheme, and dither about possibilities but never settle on a decision or course of action?

Now that you have a better understanding of excessive worry, use the next exercise to apply this knowledge to your worry experience. Your answers to these questions will be helpful in completing the worry assessment in the next section.

Exercise: Personal Reflections on Worry

Think back to the last time you experienced a significant bout of worry. Briefly state what you were concerned about.

My worry concern: _____

_____

The following questions refer to the six features of irresistible worry. Answer each question to determine if your worry concern has any of these features.

1. Were you thinking about uncertainty, the possibility that something bad could happen in the future? List the what-if thoughts that occurred during the worry episode.

    _____

    _____

2. Did the worry feel uncontrollable? Did you keep telling yourself not to worry?

    _____

    _____

3. Did your world and future appear negative and threatening? If so, in what way? What were you thinking would be so bad about the future?

    _____

    _____

4. Write down whether you used any of the ineffective control strategies listed in tables 2.1 and 2.2.

    _____

    _____

5. Do you believe the worry was beneficial in any way? If so, note what was positive about worrying.

_____

_____

6. Did the worry result in any decision or course of action? If not, what was the outcome of your worry?

_____

_____

Were many of the six features present in your worry concern? If so, then you likely experienced excessive or irresistible worry. You'll want to continue doing the exercises in this chapter to learn more effective strategies to dial back worry.

Worry Assessment

A better understanding of worry is important, but you'll also want to assess whether your worry is a chronic form of RNT. We start by exploring the nature and extent of your worry concerns.

Exercise: The Worry Domains Checklist

Seven life domains relevant to worry are listed below. Place a checkmark beside each domain that is associated with worry. In the space provided, briefly state what you are worried about. Review your responses to the Identify Negative Experiences and Thoughts exercise from chapter 1 for suggestions on worry themes.

☐ Performance, evaluation, or security of work or school. State worry concern:

_____

☐ Lack of, poor quality, or instability of intimate or family relationships. State worry concern:

_____

☐ Uncertain or aimless future. State worry concern:

_____

☐ Financial matters. State worry concern:

_____

☐ Safety concerns, such as injury to self or significant others. State worry concern:

_____

☐ Illness or threats to health of self, family, or close friends. State worry concern:

_____

☐ World or community events. State worry concern:

_____

☐ Minor matters (appointments, repairs, errands, and so forth). State worry concern:

_____

Were most of your worries concentrated in one or two life domains? If you didn't check any of the above life domains, it's unlikely worry is a problem for you. The more life domains you checked, the greater the likelihood that worry contributes to your distress.

The Worry Domains Checklist indicates whether your worry is specific to one issue or a general response to many life domains. The checklist is also useful for highlighting your main worry concerns. The next step is to assess how you experience worry. You can refer back to your answers on the Personal Reflections on Worry worksheet to help with the next exercise.

Exercise: Worry Domain Evaluation

Below are seven key statements about the worry experience. Review your work in the last two exercises and circle "Yes" if the statement applies to your general experience of worry.

Statements		
1. I have worries in several life domains.	Yes	No
2. My worry concerns are clearly exaggerated.	Yes	No
3. Some of my worries are about minor matters of little personal significance.	Yes	No
4. My worry is rarely helpful in resolving the problem or situation.	Yes	No
5. Many of my worries focus on problems I didn't create and are outside my control.	Yes	No
6. Often I start worrying about a single issue, but then it spreads to other concerns like a chain reaction.	Yes	No
7. As I review these life domains, I realize my worries are excessive.	Yes	No

Did you endorse most of the statements? If so, it's likely you're experiencing excessive or maladaptive worry. Rather than making progress on your life problems, you're likely getting stuck in worry. This will cause you to feel anxious and helpless to deal with life's adversities.

Fortunately, there are strategies you can use to overcome excessive worry. Before we get to these strategies, it's important to distinguish between worries caused by real-life problems and worry related to more improbable, even hypothetical, personal catastrophes.

The Two Faces of Worry

We worry most about future problems that are unpredictable, somewhat novel, and associated with a serious negative consequence for self or loved ones. There are two types of worry. One is "reality-based worry," which concerns problems or situations occurring in the here and now over which you have some control or influence. Life can be hard, so you may worry about very real problems, difficulties, and uncertainties. Liam had several realistic worries, like getting top marks on his exams, his persistent stomach pain and headaches, as well as his difficulty sleeping.

Worry about real-life problems is not always maladaptive. Sometimes worry helps us discover an action that solves the problem. For chronic worriers, however, RNT about life's problems is ineffective, causing failure in problem-solving skills (Leahy 2005).

A second type of worry is more "imaginative." It focuses on hypothetical problems that are only remotely possible. It's unproductive because it also deals with exaggerated threat over which we have little control. Often imaginative worry is speculative, like, *What if I get sick? What if I don't get the job promotion?* or *What if my teenage son gets charged for drunk driving?* The strategies most effective for reducing worry depend on whether your concerns are about current, realistic problems or distant, speculative possibilities. The next exercise will help you determine which type of worry is most relevant for you.

Exercise: Worry Type Checklist

Review the worries you listed on the Worry Domains Checklist. Write down your most common worries in the space provided.

1. _____

2. _____

3. _____

Below is a checklist of the main features of realistic versus imaginative worry (Leahy 2005). Place a checkmark beside statements that are most relevant to the three worries you listed.

Realistic Worry	Imaginative Worry
☐ The worry deals with a current, real-life problem.	☐ The worry deals with unanswerable or implausible scenarios.
☐ I have some influence over the outcome.	☐ I have minimal or no influence over the outcome.
☐ I can think about a range of possible outcomes that vary in degree of negative consequence.	☐ I tend to focus on a single, catastrophic outcome even though it is highly unlikely.
☐ I can accept (tolerate) some uncertainty and risk.	☐ I get preoccupied with details about how the worst outcome could happen.
☐ I can accept an imperfect solution.	☐ The solution needs to be perfect.
☐ The primary concern of the worry is problem solving rather than anxiety or distress reduction.	☐ The primary concern is reduction of anxiety or distress.
☐ Some decision or course of action could be taken to deal with the problem.	☐ I need to reach a certain level of control and certainty over the problem.
☐ I feel confident in my ability to deal with the worry concern.	☐ I feel helplessness and not confident in my ability to cope with the worry concern.

If you checked more statements in the left column, then it's likely that you're worrying about current, real-life difficulties. You'll find the problem-solving intervention most appropriate for this type of worry. If you checked more statements in the right column, then your worry is about more distant, speculative matters. The decatastrophizing and worry exposure interventions are more appropriate for this type of worry.

Effective Problem Solving

Problem solving is the most effective strategy for worry about realistic life problems. Liam had weekly tests and assignments that required intense preparation. Doing poorly on an exam was a real possibility that could jeopardize his chances for medical school. This caused Liam to worry about whether he was studying enough, whether he knew the material, and the possible outcome of each exam. One way Liam could reduce his test-taking worry was to view it as a problem to be solved. There are several steps to the problem-solving approach that can shift your mindset from worry to planned action.

Step 1. Evaluate Personal Responsibility and Control

Taking charge of a problem begins with knowing the limits of your influence over the situation. Responsibility is the extent that you played a significant role in creating the problem, and control is how much influence you have in determining a desired outcome. The problem-solving approach works best for problems involving moderate responsibility and control.

We don't have absolute responsibility or control over most of our worrisome problems. Normally, responsibility and control are limited to certain aspects of a problem. You'll need a good understanding of where you stand with a problem before you put a plan into action. Liam knew he had limited control in determining what his professors thought of him, but he had more control and responsibility over his study habits. Thus, personal responsibility and control were greater for his academic performance than for what others thought of him. The next exercise provides a method to evaluate your level of responsibility and control over the realistic problems driving your worry.

Exercise: Personal Responsibility and Control Assessment

Write in the space provided a real-life problem that's causing you to worry.

Real-life worry problem: _____

_____

Next, use a blank sheet of paper to list everything that caused, maintained, or created conse-quences related to this real-life problem. This should include all your actions and decisions, those of others, and any external factors. Use the columns below to categorize each item in your list as primarily under your responsibility and control or primarily outside your responsibility and control.

Aspects of Worry Problem Under My Responsibility and Control	Aspects of Worry Problem Outside My Responsibility and Control
1.	1.
2.	2.
3.	3.
4.	4.

Based on your responses, how much overall responsibility and control do you have for this problem? Draw a vertical line through the bar to indicate the percentage of personal responsibility and control.

0%	50%	100%
Responsibility & Control	Responsibility & Control	Responsibility & Control

What does the bar tell you about how much personal responsibility and control you have over your problem? If your estimate is above 50 percent, then the problem-solving approach is relevant for your worry concern. If your estimate is below 50 percent, consider skipping the rest of this section so you can focus on more relevant strategies like decatastrophizing and worry exposure. You can download and print copies of this exercise at http://www.newharbinger.com/45052.

Step 2. Define the Problem

It is important to have realistic goals or desired outcomes for the worry-related problem. Often, we fail to make headway on life problems because we have unrealistic expectations. Liam believed he'd stop feeling anxious and worried about his health if he stopped having nausea and stomach pains. But this was unrealistic because Liam had little control over the occurrence of these unwanted abdominal sensations. Instead, he needed to redefine the problem as "learning to live with nausea and stomach pain so they cause the least amount of distress and interference in daily living."

Like Liam, you may have unrealistic expectations about your worry-related problem that makes it impossible for you to do anything about it. Instead, identity a middle step that you can control and that moves you closer to a better outcome than the present situation. Consider the following examples of real-life problems that can easily generate worry and how each can be redefined as a workable problem.

Example #1	
Real-life worry:	*Just been diagnosed with a serious chronic illness and worried about premature death.*
Redefine as:	*I need to learn what changes to make in my lifestyle and how to live with this chronic illness.*
Example #2	
Real-life worry:	*Stuck in a job I hate and worried I'll never find more satisfying employment.*
Redefine as:	*I need to rethink my job search strategy and make changes to my written, online, and in-person presentation.*
Example #3	
Real-life worry:	*Suspicious and worried that my marriage will end in divorce because my partner is having an affair.*
Redefine as:	*Consider how to change my communication style in order to deal more effectively with our relationship problems.*

Use the following worksheet to redefine your problem-based worry in a more realistic manner.

Exercise: Problem Redefinition

In the space provided, briefly describe the real-life problem and dreaded outcome that worries you most.

My real-life problem worry: _____

_____

_____

Next, write down how you can redefine the problem in terms of some decision or action you could take that is within your control and would help you achieve a better outcome. Consider the following questions when redefining the problem.

- What could I do differently that would be a positive step toward dealing with this problem?

- What am I able to do about the problem at this moment?

- How can I cope with this problem differently?

- What do I have control over, and what do I just need to accept?

- What are more realistic goals or expectations regarding this problem?

- What are the costs and benefits of seeing the problem in terms of what I can work on right now?

My redefined real-life problem: _____

_____

_____

_____

_____

Liam's redefined real-life problem:

I can't stop the nausea and stomach pain, but I can make sure I'm eating right and getting exercise. When these sensations occur, I can use some simple pain management strategies to sit with the pain and ride it out. I'll continue to study, go to class, and interact with people regardless of what my stomach's doing. I know it's a common stress reaction, and it'll go as quickly as it comes. I need to keep a cool head about it and not catastrophize.

Were you able to construct a more realistic, workable perspective on the worry problem? If you are struggling with this exercise, seek help from a close friend, family member, or therapist. It will be difficult to use the problem-solving approach if you are focused on outcomes that are beyond your control.

Step 3. Take Action

This step involves implementing the course of action you've developed in the last step. You'll want to write out the various steps in your action plan. This involves specifying where, when, and how you will conduct each step in the plan. Also, you can use the next worksheet to log everything you've done to put the plan into action.

Exercise: Track Your Actions

List the specific steps of the action plan based on your redefinition of the real-life problem. Use a blank sheet to list additional steps if needed. You can also download and print copies of this worksheet at http://www.newharbinger.com/45052.

Step 1:	Step 2:
Step 3:	Step 4:
Step 5:	Step 6:
Step 7:	Step 8:
Step 9:	Step 10:

Next, record the actions you've taken in your daily life to follow the plan.

Date	Actions Taken to Implement Plan	How Action Succeeded or Failed

Liam's redefined goal was to adopt a more accepting attitude toward his nausea and stomach pain. To achieve this goal, he broke it down into the following steps:

1. Discover foods that irritate my GI system and remove them from my diet.

2. Keep a daily schedule and adopt a more balanced lifestyle.

3. Don't overstudy because of worry and anxiety about exams.

4. Build relaxation and enjoyment into my daily activities.

5. Maintain a regular schedule even when feeling stomach discomfort.

6. Practice simple pain management and refocusing strategies when in pain.

7. Correct exaggerated negative thinking about the stomach pain and nausea.

Step 4. Evaluate Your Success

It's important to evaluate whether the plan you implemented in the last step is effective. You'll want to review the Track Your Actions worksheet to determine your success with implementation. You'll need specific indicators to know whether a course of action was effective. Ask yourself:

• Did I follow through with all the steps in my plan of action?

• Were some steps more difficult than others?

• Did I spend enough time implementing the plan, or did I procrastinate?

• Are there some steps in the plan that need to be changed to make them more helpful?

Liam did some reading on stress-related nausea and stomach pain. He kept a food diary and discovered that some foods tend to upset his stomach more than others. He also set up a regular fitness schedule with a couple of friends. He kept to a more reasonable study schedule to curb his tendency to overprepare and reached out to some former friends to increase his social life. He rated his nausea and stomach pain daily, taking note of his ability to tolerate the symptoms while carrying on with life as usual. However, Liam had trouble correcting his negative thinking about the symptoms, so he decided to seek help from a cognitive behavior therapist. Like Liam, you may need to make some changes to your plan. No doubt you'll discover that problem solving is one of the best strategies for curbing worry about real-life problems.

Decatastrophize the Worry

All worry is repetitive thinking about worst-case scenarios. The imagined catastrophe could be an immediate possibility, or it could be a remote possibility in the distant future, such as *Will I die young? What if no one likes me? What if I run out of money and become destitute? What if there is no meaning to life? What if I am condemned to hell?* This is not to say these "imaginative" concerns are unimportant or pure fiction. They are worst-case possibilities, but they're often distant events outside our sphere of control. There are things we can do to live healthfully, save for retirement, and nurture meaningful relationships. But these actions don't eliminate the possibility of major calamity, like serious illness, death, or financial ruin. For this reason, decatastrophizing is a better way to deal with imaginative worry than problem solving. There are four phases to this strategy.

Phase 1. Discover the Catastrophe

Decatastrophizing starts with identifying the imagined worst-case scenario, or catastrophe, at the heart of your worry. One of Liam's imagined catastrophes was that his marks would drop due to stress and worry. As a result, he'd fail to get into medical school and then spend the rest of his life feeling defeated, worthless, and depressed. Another imagined catastrophe was a fear of being so driven to excel in university that he ends up alone, dependent on his parents and lacking friends or meaningful relationships.

Review the worries you listed in the Worry Domains Checklist and select one that is frequent, distressing, and related to some distant dreaded possibility. Write this *imaginative worry* in the space provided.

My imaginative worry: _____

_____

_____

_____

Liam's imaginative worry:

I am thirty-five years old and living a lonely pathetic life devoid of purpose or meaning because I'm stuck in a low-paying, mundane job. I'm living a wasted life characterized by failure, weakness, and shame. This is all because I could never recover from failing to get into medical school.

What is the worst possible outcome that's driving your worry? To understand the fear at the core of your worry, it's important to write a detailed account of the catastrophic outcome you imagine could happen. The next exercise will help you write out a full description of your worry catastrophe.

Exercise: The Catastrophic Narrative

Write a description of what your life would be like if the catastrophic outcome happened. The description should be at least a half of a page in length. Try to elaborate on the causes and consequences of the catastrophe to you, your family, friends, and others. The following questions will help you describe your catastrophic narrative.

- What do you imagine caused the catastrophe? Who was responsible for it?

- What negative effect does it have on your mood, actions, social relations, physical health? What effect does it have on your loved ones?

- What is the likelihood the catastrophe will happen? Do you think you could bear it?

- Do you imagine having any control over the catastrophe? How might you try to cope with it?

- How would your life be ruined or changed for the worst if the catastrophe happened?

My catastrophic narrative: _____

_____

_____

_____

_____

_____

_____

_____

_____

Use a blank sheet of paper if you need more space. If you're struggling to write a narrative or you're unsure whether you are thinking in a catastrophic way, you could ask for help from someone who knows about your worries, such as a partner, parent, close friend, or therapist. The effectiveness of decatastrophizing depends on having a full description of your most dreaded worry outcome.

Phase 2. Evaluate the Catastrophe

Catastrophizing is what makes repetitive worry so distressing. But this type of thinking is an exaggeration of reality that assumes you'll be overwhelmed by the dreaded outcome. Research indicates that 85 percent of our worries don't turn out as badly as we think, and when a negative outcome occurs, most of us (79 percent) are much better at coping with it than we expected (Borkovec, Hazlett-Stevens, and Diaz 1999). So, let's put your catastrophic thinking under the microscopic, test it out, and discover a more balanced, realistic possible outcome than the imagined catastrophe. A therapeutic strategy called "cognitive restructuring" is an effective way to correct unhelpful thinking like catastrophizing (Beck and Emery 1985).

There are four main elements to cognitive restructuring of catastrophic worry: (a) gather evidence for and against the catastrophe happening, (b) evaluate your coping ability, (c) identify thinking errors, and (d) conduct behavioral experiments in which catastrophic predictions are tested in real time. Table 3.1 presents the most common cognitive errors found in worry.

Take, for example, a cognitive restructuring approach to Liam's catastrophic fear that he'll fail to get into medical school and end up a miserable, pathetic loser for the rest of his life. It starts with evidence that many aspiring premed students fail to get into medical school, so Liam could do some research on what happens to these individuals. What's the evidence for the catastrophe, that students are doomed to a life of misery if they fail to attain their dream of medical school? Is there evidence that contradicts the catastrophe? For example, does he know of family members or acquaintances who had a significant career disappointment and yet managed to live a very satisfying, meaningful life? Also, is there evidence that he's better able to deal with disappointment than expected? What other major life goals could he attain whether or not he's a medical doctor? Could he not still have a loving intimate relationship, be a devoted father, have many friends, maintain good health, earn a comfortable living, travel worldwide, and make a significant contribution to his community without a career in medicine? As Liam examines his catastrophic thinking, he's able to see several errors in his thinking, like jumping to conclusions, fortune-telling, and all-or-nothing thinking. This reanalysis of his catastrophic thinking could lead Liam to an alternative perspective: *There is far more to a fulfilled life than being a medical doctor. I need to see my future more broadly and focus on all aspects of living that contribute to happiness and life satisfaction. Failing to get accepted into medical school would be a challenging but not impossible disappointment to overcome.* The next exercise presents a worksheet to help you use cognitive restructuring on your catastrophic narrative.

Table 3.1. *Common Thinking Errors in Worry*

Error, Distortion	Definition	Example
Overestimate threat	You create a high expectation that the worst possible outcome is more likely to happen than is realistically probable.	When your teenage son is past his curfew, you assume he's been in a car accident.
Jumping to conclusions	When you think something is not right, you conclude that the worst will happen without thinking about how this could happen.	You assume you're in trouble because you're asked to meet with human resources.
Emotional reasoning	You assume that being anxious means there's a greater likelihood the worst outcome will happen.	You feel anxious about flying, so you assume that flying must be dangerous.
Fortune-telling	You make negative predictions about the future as if you can foresee the future.	You're worried about making a presentation and assume you'll do a terrible job.
All-or-nothing	You consider threat and safety in rigid, absolute terms as either all present or all absent.	If there is occasional tension, our marriage is threatened, but if we always get along, our marriage must be fine.
Personalization	You assume excessive responsibility or completely blame yourself for negative events.	You have a difficult child and assume that it's due to your "bad" parenting.

Exercise: Cognitive Restructuring

Read over your Catastrophic Narrative and write in bullet form all the reasons (evidence) that indicate this worst-case outcome is quite likely to happen. Next, write down all the reasons that suggest the worst-case outcome is much less likely to happen than you think. Repeat the exercise for evidence or reasons for and against your ability to cope with the worst outcome if it happened. You can draw on any information you've encountered, your past experiences, or the experiences of other people.

Evidence For & Against Likelihood the Catastrophe Will Happen	Evidence For & Against My Personal Ability to Cope with the Catastrophe
Evidence for it happening:	Evidence I couldn't cope:
Evidence against it happening:	Evidence I could cope:

List thinking errors evident in your catastrophic thinking (see table 3.1): _____

_____

What could you do that would test your ability to cope with some negative aspect of the worry concern?

_____

_____

After completing this exercise, were you surprised to find that the evidence for your worry catastrophe was rather flimsy? Were you exaggerating the likelihood that it could happen? Was there considerable evidence that you could deal with the worst outcome (catastrophe) better than you assumed? Cognitive restructuring is the most important element of decatastrophizing, so you'll likely want to spend extra time with this exercise. Visit http://www.newharbinger.com/45052 to download and print copies of this exercise.

If your work on cognitive restructuring was successful, you'll realize that the way you've been thinking about your worry concern is full of errors and false assumptions. Catastrophizing feeds runaway worry. Take a moment to review some of the characteristics of RNT in chapter 1. Can you see how catastrophic thinking causes RNT, making your worry intense, persistent, and uncontrollable? The final phase in decatastrophizing involves creating a more realistic, balanced alternative to catastrophic thinking.

Phase 3. Develop an Alternative Outcome

Catastrophic thinking is a prediction. The worried person is thinking, *I better get prepared for a catastrophe because with my luck it will probably happen.* But repetitive worry doesn't lead to effective preparation. What a waste of your time and effort if the catastrophe never comes or if it's so far in the future that you'd be better off dealing with more immediate problems. To counter catastrophic predictions, you'll need to come up with a more likely, realistic outcome that's still negative but an alternative to the catastrophe. Think of several potential less-than-positive outcomes associated with your worry concern and select the outcome you think is more likely to happen. Don't sugarcoat the alternative with your most desired outcome. This won't be helpful. Instead, stick with a negative outcome that lies somewhere in the middle between a highly desired outcome and the worst possible outcome you can imagine (the catastrophe). The next exercise provides guidelines and a worksheet for creating a more balanced possible outcome that you can imagine could happen with your worry concern.

Exercise: A More Realistic Prediction

Write out a prediction or an expectation that presents a more likely, realistic negative outcome related to your worry concern. You can write this description in the space provided below, or you can type it into your phone for easy access. This alternative prediction should include the following elements.

- How the expected outcome occurred: what sequence of events led to the outcome.

- The consequence of the outcome: how it affected you or others in your family immediately and in the long term.

- How you coped with the outcome: what you did to manage this more realistic but undesirable turn of events.

- How you accepted the uncertainty of the outcome: that you were not overwhelmed by the sudden and unexpected occurrence of the negative event.

My alternative outcome: _____

_____

_____

_____

_____

_____

_____

_____

Did you have difficulty thinking of an alternative, more realistic scenario to your catastrophic worry? If so, consider Liam's alternative to his repetitive worry about a decline in his academic performance that would sabotage his dream of being a medical doctor and lead him into a wasted, miserable, and pointless life.

Liam's alternative scenario:

All students face an uncertain future. It can be no other way because the future is unknowable. I can only do my best academic work, but it may not be enough. The door to medical school may close, and like millions of young people, I'll need to deal with a major disappointment in my life. I'll need to look for other ways to attain purpose, meaning, and fulfillment. Maybe I'll find it in my most intimate and important relationships or in an equally challenging career in science or business. Many people outside medicine have a "life well lived," and many within medicine live unfulfilled and depressing lives. My happiness depends on so much more than medicine. But for now, I can only do my best because there is nothing more than one's best. The future is unknown and full of uncertainty. I have no choice but to do my best, accept uncertainty, resolve disappointment, and adopt a broader perspective on happiness.

Effective Use of Decatastrophizing

Decatastrophizing is most effective when you practice it regularly. Doing it once is not enough! Each time you worry, you'll want to return to your decatastrophizing work, revising and adding to your answers when you have new information or a different worry experience. Correcting your catastrophic thinking is not simply a matter of reciting the alternative narrative. Instead, you will need to drill deeply into why the catastrophic thinking is unrealistic and why the alternative is the more likely outcome. Remember, in many cases our worry concerns never materialize.

But maybe you're still stuck in catastrophic thinking. You realize the alternative outcome is more likely, but you're afraid to let go of the catastrophic outcome. Maybe you still believe you'll be better prepared if you dwell on the absolute worst possible outcome. If so, then write out how you would cope with this catastrophe. Most of us are better at coping with negative, stressful experiences than we think. In chapter 2 you learned that letting go of control over repetitive negative thinking, like worry, is critical to improving control over this type of thinking. The three-phase decatastrophizing approach can help you let go of unsuccessful efforts to control worry.

The Worry Exposure Intervention

Worry is a way of avoiding our most intense fears. As a worrier, you know it's not an effective avoidance strategy because you still end up feeling anxious. Because of this avoidance function, facing your worry in a systematic and controlled manner is a highly effective way to reduce worry frequency and intensity. The next exercise explains how to face your worry.

Exercise: Systematic Worry Exposure

Schedule a daily thirty-minute exposure session for at least two weeks. It's best to do this at a regular time each day. You'll need a quiet, comfortable location where you won't be interrupted. You'll also want to keep your Catastrophic Narrative handy as a reminder of how to make yourself worry. The following guidelines will help you focus deeply on the worry catastrophe.

- Begin the session with five minutes of slow, deep, rhythmic, and self-focused breathing so you clear your mind of the day's concerns and activities.

- Bring the worry concern to your mind using the Catastrophic Narrative. Think deeply on the worry and its worst outcome.

- Focus your mind on every detail of the worry: what caused the imagined catastrophe, how you were to blame, and its immediate and long-term effects on you and your loved ones.

- Pay attention to feelings of anxiety and distress associated with the worry. Notice how you are making yourself feel worse as you become immersed in the worry.

- If your mind wanders during the worry session, gently bring your attention back to the worry theme.

- At the end of thirty minutes, stop the worry session. If you feel like you still want to do more worrying, save it for another day.

- End the session with another five minutes of relaxed breathing.

- Plan to engage in some activity or task after the worry session.

Use the worksheet below to record the quality of your worry exposure session. You will also find this worksheet at the website for this book: http://www.newharbinger.com/45052. Write down the date, the duration of the session, and your worry content. Then indicate how clearly you recalled the worry and the average level of distress you experienced during the exposure session. Use a 0-to-10 scale to rate your recall ability, where 0 is you were unable to generate worry and 10 is your experience of worry was identical to the times you spontaneously worry. Use a 0-to-10 scale to rate your average distress level, where 0 indicates no distress during the session and 10 indicates being as distressed as when you worry naturally.

Date of Session	Duration of Session (minutes)	Worry Content During Imaginal Exposure	Quality of Worry Recall (0 to 10)	Average Distress Level (0 to 10)

After two weeks of worry exposure, review your entries in the chart. Were you able to think catastrophically and have a vivid worry experience? Did your level of distress decline the more often you made yourself worry? Most people find that with time, they become bored with the worry. The worry experience will lose its sting when you take control and force yourself to think repeatedly about the worry concern.

Systematic exposure is another powerful strategy for learning to let go of repetitive worry. If you practice daily, you'll probably see a decline in worry distress within a few days. When worry occurs outside the exposure session, write down any new worry thoughts so you can add this new material to your worry session. It's important to remind yourself to save your worries for the scheduled exposure session later in the day. If you are getting more anxious and worried despite two weeks of repeated exposure sessions, stop the exercise and consult with your therapist or a qualified mental health professional.

Wrap-Up

In this chapter you learned:

- Worry is an excessive preoccupation with the possibility of a negative outcome related to an important life goal or task.

- Worry becomes a problem when there's heightened intolerance of uncertainty, uncontrollability, selective attention to threat, reliance on ineffective control responses, acceptance of positive and negative worry beliefs, and failed problem solving.

- There are two types of worry: one that is concerned with current, realistic problems and the other that focuses on more hypothetical, distant issues.

- A five-step problem-solving strategy is one of the most effective interventions for worry that's related to a current, realistic problem.

- Catastrophic thinking is at the heart of repetitive, imaginative worry. Decatastrophizing is one of the most effective strategies for this type of worry. It involves identifying, evaluating, and correcting a catastrophic prediction and then replacing it with a more realistic, probable expectation.

- Worry exposure is another effective strategy for repetitive worry. It is a systematic, self-controlled approach to worry that counters fear and avoidance of the imagined catastrophe.

What's Next?

Problem solving, decatastrophizing, and worry exposure are strategies for reducing repetitive negative thoughts, or worry, about the future. But the future is not the only temporal dimension that can be overwhelmed with negativity. We can easily turn our attentional negativity to the past and become negatively preoccupied with what happened to us. When this happens, we shift from the relentless what-ifs of worry to the persistent why questions of rumination.

CHAPTER 4

• • • • •

Interrupt Rumination

Maybe your repetitive negative thoughts aren't about the future but rather some past disappointment. You keep asking yourself, *Why did this happen to me?* Or, *Why can't my life be different?* This relentless questioning of the past is called *rumination*, and it is another common form of RNT. Just as worry leads to anxiety, rumination contributes to sadness and depression. Rumination is a lot like worry, except that it focuses on past negative experiences and is concerned about our failure to reach important life goals and desires (Watkins 2016).

Is there something in your past that you can't stop thinking about? Is there a major disappointment, loss, failure, or other difficulty and you keep wondering why it happened and how badly it's affected your life? Are you now feeling depressed, discouraged, or hopeless? We can become preoccupied with almost any negative experience. Consider the following examples.

- Your annual work evaluation is just lukewarm.

- You experience loss or a breakup of a valued relationship.

- You're diagnosed with a serious medical condition.

- You experience a significant career disappointment or setback.

- You've been feeling depressed for a long time.

Not all rumination is the same. It can vary in length and intensity. You know that being stuck in the past is bad for your mental health, but you can't break free. The preoccupation with the past is distracting you from important present-day concerns, and it's driving you further into discouragement and despair. In this chapter, you'll learn about strategies that can turn defeat into victory over repetitive rumination.

Like most people, you may have a commonsense understanding of rumination. This is fine for everyday conversation. But a more specific, science-based understanding of rumination is needed to use the exercises and worksheets presented in this chapter. So, we begin with Maria's story, which illustrates the link between rumination and depression. You'll then learn about two types of rumination and how to determine whether your persistent thoughts of the past qualify as excessive rumination. The rest of the chapter provides instruction on three rumination-busting strategies that work by diverting your attention from the past to the present.

Maria's Story: Trapped in Rumination

Maria struggled with repeated bouts of depression that could last several months. In the past few years, the depressions were recurring more rapidly. Maria was placed on a variety of antidepressants that helped, but she never achieved a symptom-free state. On a couple of occasions, Maria had to go on short-term disability. Although she had a successful career, Maria's life had not gone as she hoped. She was involved in a couple of serious long-term romantic breakups that left her brokenhearted. She was becoming more hesitant about intimacy in her life and had some disastrous experiences with online dating. She was finding it hard to make friends, so her social life was stagnant. She did little else but work and spent most evenings and weekends alone at home. She gained weight because of poor diet and little exercise. All told, Maria hated her life and berated herself for being unable to pull herself together.

When depressed, Maria experienced a relentless barrage of "why" questions. Why do I keep getting depressed? Why can't I just snap out of it? Why am I so lazy and unable to motivate myself to do anything on weekends? Why have I not fallen in love? Did I make a mistake breaking up with the last guy? Why don't men find me attractive? Why do I have no friends? *Maria could spend hours caught in vicious cycles of "why thinking" that made her feel more depressed, anxious, and hopeless about her future. She never arrived at any answer to the why questions. In fact, the years of rumination led her to a devastating conclusion: she was a weak, worthless individual who was incapable of living a full and interesting life.*

Two Types of Rumination

Rumination looks a lot like worry. They are both negative, repetitive, uncontrollable, and passive forms of thinking. Many people experience both types of negative thought. Yet, there are several important differences between them. Rumination focuses on the past, takes the form of why questions, and tends to be associated with depression. Worry has a future orientation, takes the form of what-if, and is associated with anxiety.

Like worry, rumination can be helpful if done the right way. For example, imagine you're looking for work and you've just had a poor job interview. You could repeatedly think about that experience, try to understand what you did wrong, and how it could be corrected in the future. This would be a helpful form of rumination. It does not focus on, *Why did I mess up the interview?* or *I'll never get a good job*, but instead concentrates on how you could improve your interview skills. With helpful rumination, we quickly shift from a focus on the past to dealing with present concerns. This type of rumination helps us reach desired personal goals. It provides new insights into improving our current situation. In this chapter, you'll learn how to transform excessive, maladaptive rumination into its more helpful counterpart.

There are two types of maladaptive rumination. One is *emotion-focused rumination*, which centers on the causes and consequences of being depressed (Nolen-Hoeksema 1991). The second is *stress-reactive rumination*, which focuses on the causes and consequences of stressful life events. Maria had both types of rumination. Sometimes she got stuck in trying to figure out why she kept getting depressed and what it meant for her life in the future (*emotion-focused rumination*). At other times, she'd ruminate on past breakups and why she had difficulty developing an intimate relationship (*stress-reactive rumination*). If you ruminate, do you spend most of the time trying to figure out why bad things have happened or why you've fallen short of your life goals (stress-reactive rumination)? Or are you preoccupied with the causes and consequences of your depression or anxiety (emotion-focused rumination)? Regardless of your type of rumination, you'll want to spend time with the next exercises because they provide a foundation for the three rumination reduction strategies.

Exercise: Identify Your Rumination Concerns

Recall the last few times you've been caught in a rumination cycle—that is, a relentless cycle of why questions. Are there common themes or issues in your thinking? Were you thinking about how you felt (for example, depressed) or about a certain past stressful event? Write a brief description of each rumination concern in the relevant space.

Emotion-focused rumination concern: _____

_____

_____

_____

Stress-reactive rumination concern: _____

_____

_____

_____

_____

Is your rumination more about being depressed, or are your thoughts about some past disappointment? Do you have more than one rumination concern? If so, use extra paper to record all of them. It's okay if you were able to think of only one type of rumination. You can leave the irrelevant type blank. Some people have only one type of rumination. If you had trouble recalling a rumination concern, consider observing your depressive moments over the next week and write down what you are repeatedly thinking. Do you see any rumination in your negative thoughts? If so, which type?

Rumination Assessment

We are more likely to ruminate when depressed. So, it's important to determine whether rumination plays a significant role in your depressed moods. The next exercise covers the main features of rumination. You'll be able to determine the intensity of your rumination and whether it's excessive based on your score. The twenty items focus on three aspects of rumination: a repetitive style of thinking, brooding, and positive beliefs about rumination.

Exercise: Ruminative Experience Scale

Place a checkmark under the scale value that indicates how well each item describes your rumination beliefs and experiences. Refer to the emotion-focused and stress-reactive rumination concerns you wrote down earlier to refresh your memory about rumination experiences. Use the following score key:

0 = does not describe my rumination experiences/beliefs

1 = slightly describes my rumination experiences/beliefs

2 = moderately describes my rumination experiences/beliefs

3 = strongly describes of my rumination experiences/beliefs

4 = exactly describes my rumination experiences/beliefs

Statements When ruminating...	0	1	2	3	4
1. I think about the problem for a long period of time, but it never leads to greater clarity or understanding.					
2. I wonder what I did to deserve these problems or my unfortunate situation.					
3. I believe it keeps me focused on my personal goals and values.					
4. I become highly self-critical, wondering why I can't deal with things more effectively.					
5. I believe it helps me discover why negative things are happening to me.					
6. I'm unable to resolve the problem or find a solution no matter how much I think about it.					
7. I tend to imagine alternative scenarios that could have led to a better outcome.					
8. I believe I gain deeper meaning and understanding.					

Statements When ruminating...	0	1	2	3	4
9. I do a lot of wishful thinking about how things could have turned out better.					
10. I'm reminded that it's important to think through your difficulties.					
11. I get so consumed in my thinking about a problem that nothing distracts me.					
12. I often compare myself to others and wonder why I seem to be worse off.					
13. I think how it helps me prevent future mistakes and failures.					
14. My mind goes over the same concerns again and again, especially when I'm distressed.					
15. I'm thinking that improvements can't be made until I have a complete understanding of the past.					
16. I daydream about how past events could have turned out more like my ideal outcome.					
17. I'm convinced I need to understand what is causing my depression or other distress.					
18. My mind is consumed for some time by the past.					
19. I believe it'll help me figure out a better solution to my problems.					
20. I wonder why I seem so weak and unable to cope with life's difficulties and challenges.					

Scores on the Ruminative Experience Scale can range from 0 to 80. Because the scale was developed for this workbook, we don't have cut-off scores to distinguish between excessive and normal rumination. However, the higher your score, the more likely it is you are experiencing excessive rumination. If your total score is 60 or more, it's possible that excessive rumination is a significant contributor to your distress.

What we ruminate about depends on our personality and life situation. What have you learned about your rumination? Do you have more emotion-focused or stress-reactive rumination, or some combination of the two? Did you score 60 or more on the Ruminative Experiences Scale? If so, you'll find the following rumination reduction strategies effective for repetitive thought about being depressed or some past troubling experience. If your score is under 60, the rest of the chapter can help you ruminate in a more helpful manner. Wherever you lie on the rumination scale, you've taken an important step in gaining a better understanding of how you ruminate. You're now ready to use this knowledge to change how you think about the past.

Rethink Lost Goals

Our most important life goals are the ones that provide emotional security, safety, and certainty. When our ability to attain these goals is interrupted, we might ruminate to understand what went wrong (Segerstrom et al. 2000). We've all been there in one way or another. Maybe financial security was important to you, but then for some reason your savings and investments took a terrible hit. Or maybe you place high value on family and a loving relationship, but then marital problems developed, and you found yourself estranged from your spouse and children. Or you've been conscientious in practicing a healthy lifestyle, but suddenly you're diagnosed with a serious illness. These are all common examples of disrupted goals and aspirations that create a gap between our current state and a desired outcome.

When our dreams are shattered, our attention often turns inward in an attempt to understand what went wrong. This can be healthy if it empowers you to let go of the past and deal with any current negative consequences. But often rumination becomes a feeble coping strategy aimed at trying to reclaim a lost goal. If you're caught in unhealthy rumination, you might be thinking that you'll find the reason for your failure or unfortunate life experience. You might be thinking, *If I can figure out what caused this problem, then I'll discover a solution that'll make my life better.* But repetitive thinking about the past rarely produces great revelations. Instead, it stymies our ability to deal effectively with the consequences of the past. Before we know it, we're stuck in a mental loop with no end in sight.

When ruminating, do you catch yourself rehashing the same stuff over and over? Maybe you keep asking, *Why did this happen to me? Where did I go wrong?* or you keep thinking about how your life's been ruined. We can get so caught up in the rumination that we forget what we lost—what we once desired but can no longer have because of the past difficulty. Breaking the cycle of rumination begins by rediscovering what you lost. What goal did you want to achieve but now can't reach because of past disappointments or difficulties? The next exercise will help you identify the lost goal driving your rumination and think more broadly about the reasons why you failed to reach the goal.

Exercise: Discover the Lost Goal

Think back to a lost goal or an unmet need that causes you to ruminate. Maybe it's something you wanted to achieve but didn't, a valued relationship that is no more, or good health that's been decimated by disease or injury. If you're having trouble identifying a lost goal related to your rumination, review the rumination concerns you wrote down earlier. Keeping in mind your rumination concern, do your best to answer the following questions.

- How important is the failed or disrupted goal to your overall well-being and life satisfaction? Could you ever recover some level of life satisfaction if the goal is never met? If so, what would life be like if you never achieved the goal? How does this differ from the life you originally imagined?

  _____

  _____

  _____

- Is the goal temporarily or permanently lost?

  _____

  _____

- What are the consequences to you, your family, or others of not achieving this goal?

  _____

  _____

  _____

Were you able to identify the lost goal or aspiration that's driving your rumination? Sometimes the goal disrupted by a past negative experience is obvious. For Maria, it was easy to see that having a loving relationship was an important lost aspiration that caused rumination. She believed a loving partner was necessary for happiness. But is it possible Maria was exaggerating the negative impact of being single?

Is it true a person can't be happy if they're single? Like Maria, is it possible you've been overstating the negative impact of a lost goal? Also, you may be thinking its negative effect is permanent, but is it possible that its effects on life satisfaction will dwindle with time?

Are you having difficulty with this exercise because the lost or unmet goal is not clear? Maria also ruminated about being depressed, but the goal disruption behind this rumination was harder to see. She could discover the lost goal by starting with the first exercise question and asking, *What's the connection between being depressed and life satisfaction?* If you frame the question this way, the unmet goal is easier to see. Maria couldn't believe she'd have any quality of life as long as she had bouts of depression. The difference between being depressed and not depressed was huge, and Maria could easily list the many ways depression had dashed her hopes and dreams. In response to the second question, she believed the life she so desired was permanently lost because of the years spent struggling with depression. The consequences of not beating depression affected every facet of her life, from relationships to work to her core sense of self-worth. Thinking of depression as a thief that stole her cherished dreams and life satisfaction fueled Maria's tendency to ruminate about the depression.

The only way to beat rumination is to change the way you think about a past negative experience. The first step is to understand how this experience interferes in your life and then to determine whether its effects are as bad as you've been thinking. Like Maria, you may believe that not achieving the desired goal has destroyed your ability to have any degree of happiness. But this only strengthens the rumination and prevents you from moving beyond the past and its negative consequences.

This brings us to the next step in learning to decrease rumination. It's important to think more deeply about rumination itself and whether you've gained any benefit from all the months or even years of this repetitive thinking. Are you any closer to achieving happiness by ruminating? Has the rumination helped you figure out how to close the gap between what you desired and what actually happened? The next exercise will help you consider these questions more fully.

Exercise: Rumination Insights

For the next few days set aside thirty minutes to ruminate.

Part I. Think back to the last two or three times when you were seriously stuck in rumination. Use a blank sheet of paper to write down the time and place of the rumination episode, and what you were thinking about. Writing it down will sharpen your memory of the ruminative experience. Next, consider the difference between the lost or unmet goal that's the focus of your rumination (see previous exercise) and how much of the goal you achieved. Use the space provided to write your answers.

What I desired for myself (the lost goal): _____

_____

My current situation (how much of the goal I achieved): _____

_____

Part II. In part I you identified the difference between the goal or outcome you desired and what you achieved. Next, use the following questions to consider whether rumination has helped you understand why you didn't achieve the goal.

1. How much of not reaching the goal was due to your actions or decisions? List what you did to undermine your goal. Use a blank sheet of paper to list additional reasons.

    a. _____

    b. _____

    c. _____

    d. _____

2. What about other people? How much of not reaching your goal came from the actions or decisions of others? List what they did to undermine your goal.

    a. _____

    b. _____

    c. _____

    d. _____

3. What about random causes? How much of not reaching your goal was due to events beyond anyone's control (bad luck)? List these unfortunate experiences here.

    a. _____

    b. _____

c. _____

d. _____

Part III. You've gained a deeper understanding of how a past negative experience interfered with a desired goal from the work you've done in parts I and II. Using this new understanding, list what you could do in the present to achieve some progress toward meeting your goal.

a. _____

b. _____

c. _____

d. _____

This exercise will be difficult if you don't have a clear recollection of past rumination episodes. If this happened to you, consider writing down two or three rumination experiences over the next week or two. Then you can complete the exercise based on those experiences. Visit http://www.newharbinger.com /45052 to download and print copies of this exercise.

From your work on these exercises, you've gained new sights into the causes and solutions to your unmet goal. Compare this to what you gained from prolonged periods of rumination. Did any new solutions come to mind from working on the exercise? Are you now able to see that rumination doesn't work? Research into rumination supports this conclusion. It turns out rumination is a poor coping strategy because it narrows our attention on how we think and feel rather than on more realistic problem-solving opportunities (Watkins 2016).

When ruminating, we rarely think about how the negative experience interfered in achieving important life goals. By completing the discovery and insight exercises, you've taken an important step in shifting your thinking away from rumination. It's made you more aware that you're making no headway in achieving your desired goal and in being happy by ruminating. It's time to consider changing the goal or changing how you approach the goal. Maybe you need to do both. This was Maria's situation. She'd need to shift her goal from finding true love to maximizing happiness while being a single, middle-aged professional woman. She needed a more action-oriented approach, like being more sociable, increasing her friendship network, and enriching her leisure and recreation activities. If these changes led to more dating opportunities, this would be a bonus. With this new approach, Maria would notice a decrease in rumination because she'd be spending less time alone thinking about why she was still single. Instead, she'd be spending her time discovering ways to be happy as a single woman. Like Maria, do you need a different approach to your disrupted or lost goals?

We all have specific life goals about work, family, relationships, health, community, spirituality, and the like. But our specific goals are connected to a fundamental striving for happiness, fulfillment, and life satisfaction. When ruminating, we tend to lose sight of our desire for happiness. This is the ultimate goal we lose when ruminating. The last exercise in this section asks that you reconsider how you can take a different approach to achieving greater life satisfaction (happiness) despite past disappointments and failures.

Exercise: Alternative Goal Plan

Based on the last exercise, try mapping out a plan of action that helps close the gap between your desired goal and your current situation. Rather than focus on your failure to achieve a specific goal, accept that the goal can't be reached in the way you first desired. Instead, describe what else you could do—outside of the specific goal—that would have a positive impact on your life satisfaction. You'll want to be specific on what you need to do, when, where, and how often. You can consult the problem-solving approach in the last chapter to help with this exercise.

_____

_____

_____

_____

_____

_____

_____

_____

Your action plan should list specific decisions and actions that will increase your life satisfaction. The exercises you completed in this section are designed to lead you toward an alternative plan of action. If you are having difficulty thinking about ways you can be happier despite the bad experiences of the past, ask for help from your therapist, spouse, or close friend. Once you've written out your action plan, it's important that you implement the plan. Intentions without action are pretty useless. When you're engaged in the alternative plan, you're acting against rumination and its disrupting effects on life goals. But transforming how you deal with lost goals is not the only way to reduce rumination. The next section presents a strategy for changing your style of thinking.

From "Why" to "How" Questions

Have you noticed that when you ruminate, you ask a lot of why questions: *Why did this happen to me again? Why doesn't my life ever get better? Why am I being punished? Why do I keep failing?* Rumination is all about asking why bad things happen to us, their consequence, and what it all means (Watkins 2016). So, it's not surprising that another way to reduce rumination is to replace "why" with "how." Why questions keep us stuck in rumination, whereas how questions liberate us from repetitive thoughts of the past. You learned in the previous exercises that repeatedly searching for causes rarely leads to new understanding or a resolution to a past difficulty. This is why we end up feeling more distressed and discouraged when we ruminate.

British psychologist Edward Watkins (2016) provides a treatment for rumination that focuses on shifting from the abstract why questions of rumination to concrete how-to solutions. There are three critical steps in his approach:

1. Know when you are slipping into why thinking.

2. Replace why questions with corresponding how questions.

3. Practice shifting from why to how during periods of rumination.

We'll work through these steps, beginning with an exercise to increase your awareness of when you slip into why thinking.

Exercise: Why-Question Awareness

Review your work in the previous exercises. Can you identify some common themes about the causes, consequences, or meaning found in your rumination? What are the most frequent why questions associated with these themes? Write your why questions under each category in the space provided.

1. Causes of the ruminative concern (list the questions you ask about why the negative experience happened):

    a. _____

    b. _____

    c. _____

2. Consequences of the ruminative concern (list the what-if questions, thinking about the negative effects of the undesirable past experience as well as how it could have gone much better if only certain things had not happened):

    a. _____

    b. _____

    c. _____

3. Meaning of the ruminative concern (list ways in which the negative experience has importance or significance for you):

    a. _____

    b. _____

    c. _____

Maria's rumination about being depressed illustrates how the exercise can guide you into greater awareness of why questions. When thinking back to her rumination episodes, she recalled many why questions about the causes of her depression, such as: *Why do I keep getting depressed? Is it caused by some weakness in my character? Why can't I pull myself out of these depressions? Why am I so tired and unmotivated all the time?* Then she listed all the what-if questions that flooded her mind during rumination, such as *What if this depressive episode is different, and I never get better? What if I lose my job because of the depression?* and *What if everyone abandons me because I'm such a killjoy?* Finally, she reflected more deeply on what's so important about being a person who's prone to depression. She'd think, *Maybe this is proof that I'm a weak person, maybe I'm being punished for not being more empathic and caring toward others,* or *this is what I deserve for being so selfish.* By completing this exercise, Maria could gain greater awareness of the *power of why* in fueling her rumination. Did you make the same discovery when completing the exercise? Is *why* a dominant theme when you ruminate?

The next step is to replace the why questions of rumination with more concrete, practice-based how statements. This requires that you identify specific, real-life personal effects of the past negative experience and then develop an action plan that moves you forward in the present rather than being stuck ruminating about the past. In making this shift from why to how, two questions are critical: How did this happen? and How can I do something about it? (Watkins 2016, 189).

Exercise: Replacing Why with How

Review your answers in the previous exercise and replace them with how statements using the following three-step approach.

Step 1. Write down the specific sequence of events that led to the negative experience on which you now ruminate. Refrain from assigning blame or making judgments. Instead, be as objective and accurate as possible on what actually happened that caused the negative experience.

_____

_____

_____

Step 2. List some actions and decisions you can take so you're better managing the negative effects of the ruminative concern. These changes should decrease its negative effect on you or others. This will be your plan of action that lists distinct steps you can take to deal with the concern in a more constructive manner.

_____

_____

_____

Step 3. Write down how you can understand the past negative experience in a more specific way that avoids overgeneralizing or exaggerating its significance. Think about the ruminative concern as a discrete, time-limited, situation-specific experience rather than a defining moment in your life.

_____

_____

_____

Were you able to replace your ruminative why thinking with problem-solving how questions? If you've spent a long time ruminating on a past negative event or caught in cyclical thinking about being depressed, it can be hard to shift from why questions to more constructive how-to thinking. You'll want to take more time with this exercise because it's a key strategy for interrupting rumination. Your answers in these exercises will be more helpful if you revise them after you've had a fresh round of rumination.

When Maria ruminated about being depressed, she got stuck in the why-thinking mode. To turn this into more constructive thinking, her thinking needed to focus on how she could deal more effectively with her depression. When completing step 1, Maria could list several things that make her depression worse:

When feeling blue for several days, I avoid people at work and home.

I increase binge-watching and consumption of junk food until I feel nauseous.

I procrastinate important work assignments.

Maria's work on step 2 would involve replacing her exaggerated, self-blaming rumination about being depressed with a more problem-focused plan. She could take several specific steps to reduce the negative effects of depression, like:

Make plans to socialize with family and friends, and seek out opportunities to converse with work colleagues especially when in a depressed mood.

Arrange to exercise with a friend three or four times a week.

Work on updating my online dating profile.

Maria's work on step 3 could focus on her beliefs that depression was a sign of weakness, self-pity, and low self-worth. It was hard to see it any other way, but she could change this view by reading about depression and talking to friends and family about what it means to be depressed. This could lead to several different ways to understand depression, such as:

There are many ways in which I am a strong and resourceful person whether I feel depressed some of the time or not.

Depression is always time-limited, so my times of not being depressed far outnumber my periods of depression.

Being depression-prone is a manageable condition just like other chronic health conditions.

You've learned from this exercise how to change your thinking from why to how. You realize it's important to shift from the paralysis of rumination to the concrete action plan you developed in step 2. But now you need to practice your new how-thinking style. The next exercise presents a "why-how" behavioral experiment that you can use to practice shifting your mind from the why-thinking mode of rumination to the how-thinking style (Watkins 2016).

Exercise: Mind Shifting in the Moment of Rumination

Schedule a specific time to intentionally engage in ruminative thinking for twenty to thirty minutes. Choose a place that is quiet, comfortable, and clear of interruptions. You may want to review your Why-Question Awareness and Replacing Why with How worksheets during the exercise. Practice mind shifting by following these steps.

1. Take the first five minutes to focus your mind and relax. You can do this by practicing controlled breathing that involves taking slow, deep but natural breaths. Concentrate on the physical sensations associated with breathing. When your mind wanders, gently bring it back to the physical sensations of relaxed breathing.

2. Next, recall your main ruminative concern and think deeply about it for three to five minutes. If the rumination involves a past distressing event, imagine yourself reliving that experience. If you are ruminating about being depressed, imagine what it feels like to live your most depressive day.

3. Now that you are fully engaged with your rumination, review the reasons why the ruminative concern happened that you listed on the Why-Question Awareness exercise. Imagine that these "causes" are actually happening to you. Once they are fully in your mind, shift your attention to how things actually happened that are listed in step 1 of the Replacing

Why with How exercise. Spend more time imagining specific details of what actually happened to bring about the negative experience. Hold on to the how image for five to seven minutes.

4. Repeat the previous step, but this time imagine the consequences of the ruminative concern from part 2 of the Why-Question Awareness exercise and how you can reduce these consequences as you wrote in step 2 of the Replacing Why with How exercise. Again, bring as much detail and realism to the image as possible, being especially mindful of all the ways you could reduce the negative effects of the experience that's causing your rumination.

5. Repeat step 3 for how you've interpreted or understood the ruminative concern. First think deeply of the misinterpretations you listed in part 3 of the Why-Question Awareness exercise and then imagine the more balanced, realistic interpretations you generated in step 3 of the Replacing Why with How exercise. Make sure you spend twice as much time imagining the more balanced interpretation than the misinterpretation.

Use the following worksheet to record your experience with mind shifting. Place a checkmark in the second column each time you engage in mind shifting. In the third column, rate the overall success with the mind-shift session. Use a 0-to-10 scale, where 0 is absolutely no success or the session was a complete waste, to 10, where the session was extremely successful and you were able to shift from why to how with ease. You'll want to practice this exercise repeatedly, so make copies of the blank worksheet, which can be found at http://www.newharbinger.com/45052.

Day	20-Minute Mind-Shift Session Completed	Rate Success of Mind-Shift Session (0–10)	Note Any Problems Encountered
Monday			
Tuesday			
Wednesday			
Thursday			
Friday			
Saturday			
Sunday			

The effectiveness of mind shifting depends on how much you practice. If you work at it repeatedly, you'll become more skilled at transforming your thinking from why to how. Be patient with yourself when doing this exercise. You're learning a new but difficult mental skill that is an effective way to disrupt rumination once you master it. After several attempts with mind shifting, take note of any problems you listed in the last column and think about how you might improve your experience with the exercise.

The purpose of the Mind Shifting in the Moment of Rumination exercise is to guide you toward a more productive way of thinking about past failures and difficulties that trigger rumination. But it's also important to put this new way of thinking into practice. Through this process, you'll discover new ways to cope with the negative effects of the ruminative concern that will strengthen the how-mode of thinking. For Maria, this would mean coping differently with days of depression. There are several things she could do, like schedule social activities with friends and family, keep to her exercise routine, eat regular meals, schedule an enjoyable activity, and join in conversation with coworkers. You'll find mind shifting more effective in disrupting rumination if it's backed up with real changes in behavior.

From "Inward" to "Outward"

Rumination is all about getting stuck in our head. The previous exercises are designed to help with this problem and encourage you to refocus your efforts on solving problems in the here and now. However, changing how you think is not enough. To truly defeat rumination, we also have to change our behavior. This means moving from an "inward" focus on *what I am thinking* to an "outward" focus on *what I can do.*

When we're absorbed in an activity, we experience deep involvement and total concentration on the task at hand. Being fully absorbed in an activity causes us to lose a sense of time. Athletes can become so totally absorbed in the game that even a minor injury doesn't register until the game is over. Can you recall past experiences of being intensely focused or absorbed in an activity? It could be music, acting, sport, reading, writing, a hobby, studying, or some aspect of work. Do you recall what it was like to be fully absorbed?

Getting involved in an absorbing experience is a highly effective way to interrupt rumination (Watkins 2016). An absorbing task takes all our attention so there's none left over for rumination. Of course, a mundane or repetitive task takes less attention, so there's plenty of attentional resources left for rumination. This is why we need to engage in an activity that takes all our attention—a truly absorbing activity (Watkins 2016). Often our absorbing experiences are spontaneous. We need to be more strategic if we hope to use absorbing distraction against rumination. The next exercise will help you discover what activities might qualify as absorbing tasks that you can use to interrupt rumination.

Exercise: Behavioral Absorption

Make a list of activities that you enjoy and are sufficiently demanding that they fully occupy your mind when you do them. Try to generate a list of ten to fifteen activities you can do alone, without much expense or planning. Activities that fall under hobbies, exercise, sport, recreation, leisure, arts, and other creative ventures can be sufficiently engaging to qualify as an absorbing experience. Use the worksheet to list your engaging activities and rate how much you expect to get absorbed in that activity on a 0-to-10 scale, where 0 is no absorption and 10 is total absorption.

Activity	Expected Absorption (0–10)
1.	
2.	
3.	
4.	
5.	
6.	
7.	
8.	
9.	
10.	
11.	
12.	
13.	
14.	
15.	

After generating your list of absorption activities, place an asterisk beside the top five activities associated with the highest absorption ratings and that are most enjoyable and practical to do. Engage in one of the absorbing activities when you ruminate. Vary how much you use any activity so you don't become bored and disinterested, which will reduce the activity's ability to distract you from rumination.

Rumination becomes frequent and intense when we get stuck in our head. The Behavioral Absorption exercise is designed to shut down rumination by getting us out of our head and more engaged in the external world around us. Changing the way we think about our past difficulties and refocusing on the challenges and opportunities around us are powerful tools for breaking the habit of rumination.

Wrap-Up

In this chapter you learned:

- There are two types of rumination: one focused on the causes and consequences of feeling depressed and the other on why a past negative life event occurred that dashed important goals and aspirations.

- As a common form of RNT, rumination involves goal disruption and a generalized, abstract way of thinking. Although similar to worry, rumination has a focus on past disappointments that makes it a different type of repetitive thought.

- The two factors most important to understanding rumination are its past orientation and relentless concern with trying to gain insight into the causes and consequences of an unfortunate situation.

- Change the way you think about a goal you failed to achieve in the past to what can be done to make some progress in the present.

- Learn to shift your thinking from the why questions of rumination to practical how questions that guide action planning.

- Get outside your head by focusing on an absorbing activity rather than on the futile ruminative search for answers.

What's Next?

Rumination is difficult to break, especially if you're clinically depressed. It takes time to practice the strategies presented in this chapter. If you've done all the work in this chapter but are still ruminating, consider reviewing your work with a mental health professional. As well, individuals who are significantly depressed will need the guidance and support of a therapist to get the most from this chapter.

When bad things happen to good people, rumination is one possible response. As we ruminate on these past failures and disappointments, we can slip into self-blame and guilt for missed opportunities. This leads us to another type of RNT about the past called regret. This is the topic of our next chapter.

CHAPTER 5

Move Beyond Regret

Hardly a moment goes by in our daily lives that doesn't involve a decision. Some are trivial, such as whether to lie in bed another five minutes, what to have for lunch, or which movie to watch. Other decisions are profound and have far-reaching consequences, like our job choices, a life partner, where to live, or whether to engage in recommended medical treatment. Of course, all actions and decisions are associated with outcomes. When an outcome is positive, we rejoice that the right decision was made. But when our decision leads to a negative outcome, we often experience regret. The more important the decision, the greater the regret. Interestingly, persistent regret is more often due to a missed opportunity (*I wish I had chosen a different path*) rather than with committing some grave mistake. Regret is the negative emotion we feel when we've made decisions or taken action that has had a significant negative impact on our lives.

This is a chapter about regret. It's an emotion that seems familiar to us but in many ways is more mysterious than fear or sadness. This makes it especially important to first learn about the critical features that make regret so painful and how repetitive regretful thinking fuels depression, guilt, and self-blame. Worksheets are provided to assess your experiences of regret and its repetitive thinking style. As well, you'll be shown how to use two strategies that can help you move beyond regretful thinking.

Emily's Story: Filled with Regret

Emily had everything going for her. Her childhood was practically idyllic, coming from an affluent family with loving parents, an older sister she admired, and many playmates who filled her days with fun and adventure. This continued into high school, where she was considered one of the most popular girls who seemed to have it all: beauty, intelligence, sociability, energy, confidence, and humor. All this hope and optimism continued when Emily first entered university. But things started to take a turn for the worse in her second year. Now fifteen years later, life has not turned out so well for Emily. She's married with two school-age children, working part time at a menial job, living in the suburbs cut off from family and friends, and stuck in a marriage that has become loveless and stagnant. For the past five years, she has been taking antidepressants for what her family doctor calls clinical depression.

As Emily looks back on her life, she is overcome with regrets. She regrets her decision not to finish her undergraduate degree to instead get a job that would support her husband through law school. She broke up with her first love after cheating on him with her current husband but now wonders if she made the wrong choice. When her husband decided to accept an offer from a law firm in a distant city, Emily did not protest the move even though she now hates where they are living. And when her husband wanted the children to be close in age, Emily went along with getting pregnant even though she was feeling overwhelmed with the demands of her first baby. During periods of despair, Emily thinks back to all these decisions and imagines what her life would have been like if she had finished university and pursued her career aspirations, married her first love, or even insisted that they not move so far from family and friends. When Emily dreamed of what could have been, it only made her present reality seem so much worse. It left her with a profound sense of disappointment, self-blame, and hopelessness. She had messed up her life, and now she was paying the price.

Can you relate to Emily's story? Are there important life decisions that you've made and now you're filled with regret, disappointment, and self-blame because in hindsight you made the wrong choice? If so, it may be that regretful thinking is playing an important role in your emotional distress. Even though regret is common, most people don't really understand this repetitive way of thinking about the past. So, let's begin by unpacking regret.

Unraveling Regret: Should've, Could've Thinking

Regret is literally feeling sorry for one's self. Making a personal choice requires that we forego other choices. When we later come to realize that another choice would have led to a more desirable outcome, we feel regret (Gilovich 1995; Roese et al. 2009). In other words, regret is thinking we should've done something differently. We are most likely to feel regret when our current situation is undesirable, and we take personal responsibility for failing to make a different decision that would have resulted in a better outcome. For example, Emily decided to quit university after her second year to support her husband through law school. She now regrets that decision, believing that continuing her university education would have provided a fulfilling career rather than the low-paying, part-time work she's endured for years.

Regret is not always a bad thing. If the regret motivates us to take a different course of action and we avoid getting stuck in excessive self-blame, it can be helpful. But when a past decision or action results in a highly undesirable outcome, self-blame can become overpowering. When this happens, we can get stuck in repetitive cycles of regretful thinking. When regret becomes excessive, there is a repeated focus on blaming one's self for what might have been a better outcome (Roese et al. 2009). We can call this "should've, could've thinking." It's characterized by thinking, *I should have made a different decision that would have led to a different course of action and a better outcome.*

When regretful thinking becomes repetitive, it looks a lot like rumination. Both types of thinking are highly negative, deal with past experiences, and involve considerable self-blame. If you're struggling with persistent depression, guilt, anxiety, or negative emotion more generally, consider whether both rumination and regretful thinking are important contributors to your distress (Kraines, Krug, and Wells 2017; Roese et al. 2009).

Life affords numerous opportunities for regret. The individual rights and freedoms of a democracy provide a wide scope of personal decision making, which allows us to determine the direction of our life. We make decisions about our education, careers, whom we'll marry, where we'll live, and even whether to have children. Every choice we make carries with it the possibility of regret (Gilovich 1995). But our regrets are not random. The six biggest regrets for Americans are education, career, romance, parenting, self-improvement, and leisure, whereas the lowest are finance, family, health, friends, spirituality, and community (Roese and Summerville 2005). The first six life concerns cause more regret because they're vital to our quality of life, and we think there is always a possibility of correcting a poor decision. If you think you made a bad decision about education, you can always go back to school at any age. It's never too late to get more education. The lowest regretted concerns deal with aspects of our lives that feel less open to correction. If you made a bad financial decision in the past, it can take years to recover if, indeed, you recover at all.

Regret: A Case of Buyer's Remorse

There are several characteristics of decision making that increase the chance you'll experience intense regret over your choice, a type of buyer's remorse (the sinking feeling that you made a mistake after a purchase). The more factors present, the more likely you'll experience the repetitive regretful thinking associated with depression, guilt, anxiety, and other types of personal distress.

1. *Negative outcome.* Persistent regretful thinking only occurs if a decision causes an undesirable outcome that has significant personal value. If a decision causes a highly desired outcome, our hearts are filled with rejoicing rather than regret. But we'll feel regret if we think we've made a negative judgment about something important to our current life circumstance. Emily only started to feel regret about her marital decision when tension and conflict arose in her marriage. Being caught in a loveless marriage triggered repetitive thinking about the causes of her marital unhappiness and to question her past romantic decisions.

2. *Failures of inaction.* At first, regret is most intense when we've had a mistake, but over time, the focus shifts to regret over our failures to act. We tend to focus on "regrettable failures" because it's much harder to understand why we chose not to do something that we now know would be better for us than knowing why we made a wrong decision (Gilovich 1995). Whenever we choose a course of action, it means that alternative choices were ignored or rejected. With repetitive regretful thinking, we focus more on these alternative choices or failures of action. When overwhelmed with feelings of regret, Emily would imagine what her life might have been like if she had continued the relationship with her first serious college boyfriend.

3. *Fanciful thinking.* Regret is worse when we believe there is a better alternative to what actually happened (Roese 1997). Because we can't know the future, our imagination can run wild on how much better our life would have been had we made a different decision. Examples include: *If only I had prepared more for the interview, I would have gotten my dream job. If I had bought a cheaper preowned car, I wouldn't be so financially strapped. If I'd been more sociable and outgoing in my twenties, I'd now be in a loving intimate relationship.* We are more likely to have these idealized dreams about *what could have been* when feeling depressed or experiencing a difficult life circumstance. Unfortunately, this type of thinking is unhealthy and often intensifies negative feelings of shame, guilt, and regret (Watkins 2008).

4. *False hope.* Hope is an important belief that helps us deal with difficulties and disappointments. But there is a type of false hope that can be self-defeating. It turns out that regret is more intense when we believe there's still time to correct a bad decision. This has been called "the principle that opportunity breeds regret" (Roese and Summerville 2005, 1274). It's a type of false hope because it doesn't help us cope with our difficulties. This notion that "perceived opportunity breeds regret" is one reason educational

decisions are the most common cause of regret. We can always go back to school or take online courses to correct a perceived educational deficiency. But this can be a false hope if we simply think about the opportunity but do nothing about it. On the other hand, if there is nothing you can do about a past decision, you're less likely to feel regret. Emily's regret about quitting university was much greater than having her children so close in age. She could still do something to further her education, but she couldn't change the ages of her children.

5. *Explanation deficit.* You've often heard the phrase "hindsight is 20/20." This biased way of thinking about the past is exactly what happens in regret. We feel more regretful when we're unable to justify a bad decision or past action (Connolly and Zeelenberg 2002). This happens because it's difficult to recall the reasons why you made a poor decision in the past. You now have the benefit of knowing that your past choice led to an undesirable outcome, but you didn't know this back when you made the decision. So, you think, *I should have known better,* but you're basing this judgment on your present knowledge rather than the limited knowledge you had when you made the decision. You are surrendering to the "hindsight bias," and so you feel more regretful. Alternatively, if you conclude, *I think I made the best decision with what I knew at the time,* you're less likely to have regretful thoughts.

   Emily regretted her decision to quit university because after fifteen years, she had a hard time justifying the decision. She's convinced there were other options available to her. She could have finished her undergraduate degree part time while working enough to cover daily living expenses while her husband was in law school. She now can't remember why she so quickly settled on quitting university as the solution to their immediate financial needs. In thinking about the past, Emily had fallen victim to the hindsight bias.

6. *Responsibility and control.* Regret is greater if you believe you were in control of an unfortunate decision and its negative outcome. This makes you personally responsible for the bad decision. It's hard to regret experiences that are beyond our control. If an undesirable outcome is due to external forces, you'll feel bad about the misfortunate, but you're not to blame. It's easy to see that an inflated sense of personal responsibility for a bad outcome will cause intense self-blame, which is at the heart of repetitive regret.

7. *Self-blame.* When we have doubts over a decision, regret intensifies the more we blame ourselves for making a poor choice. As her marital difficulties increased, Emily had

more doubts and uncertainty that she had made the right decision in breaking up with her first boyfriend and moving in with her current husband. The doubt and regret seemed to feed off each other. The more she doubted, the greater the regret and vice versa.

Figure 5.1 illustrates the relationship between the seven factors that cause regretful thinking and its associated distress. If none of these factors is present with a decision, thoughts of regret will be absent. But as we experience more and more of these factors, we increase the chance of experiencing intense and repetitive regret. If most of these factors are present with an important past decision, we're more likely to experience repeated thoughts of regret. We'd also expect the intensity of that regret to depend on how important the past action or decision is to our life goals and ambitions.

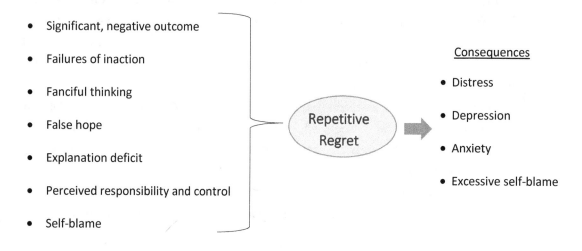

Figure 5.1. A Pathway to Repetitive Regret

Assessing Your Regrets

Given the deluge of choices in life, occasional regret is inevitable. All our decisions, even the important ones, can't be the best. Even people who are intellectually gifted have as many regrets as the average person (see Roese and Summerville 2005). So, having regrets is not a matter of intelligence or good luck. Since we can't escape regret, it's important to determine whether it's become a problem for you. We'll start with your important life concerns and determine whether a potentially regrettable decision or action is associated with that part of your life. Then we'll use a checklist based on the seven contributing factors to determine whether you are experiencing repetitive regretful thought.

Exercise: Domains of Regret

Listed below are twelve domains of living that require a range of choices, actions, and decisions. Consider each life domain and whether you have any regrets about your choices, decisions, or actions within that domain. If you have regrets, briefly state the regrettable action or decision in the second column. In the third column, briefly describe an alternative decision or action you wish you had taken that would have resulted in a better outcome today.

Life Domain	Regrettable Decision or Action	Desired (Wished-for) Decision or Action
Career		
Education		
Family		
Finance		

Life Domain	Regrettable Decision or Action	Desired (Wished-for) Decision or Action
Health		
Friends		
Parenting		
Leisure		
Community		
Romance		
Spirituality		
Self-improvement		

The twelve life domains were categories developed by Roese and Summerville (2005) in their meta-analysis of regret-ranking studies.

Were you able to recall feeling regret in one or more of the life domains? Did you have difficulty thinking of an alternative, more desirable decision or action that would have led to a better outcome? Which seems the bigger influence in your regretful thinking: the regrettable actions listed in the second column or the inaction listed in the third column? If you have persistent regret but had difficulty describing your regrets of action or inaction, consider getting help from your spouse, family member, or therapist. The regret interventions described later are based on your work in this exercise, so keep the worksheet handy. If you were unable to produce any entries even with assistance, it's possible regret is not a significant factor in your emotional distress.

One of Emily's greatest regrets overlapped with two domains: education and career. Under education, the regrettable action noted in column 2 was quitting university after her second year, and the regrettable inaction recorded in column 3 was not completing her undergraduate major in English and then pursuing a high school teaching certificate. In the career domain, her regrettable decision was accepting part-time employment as a teacher's aide, and the regrettable inaction was not obtaining her teaching qualifications even though she had preschoolers. When she felt sad and blue, Emily's regretful thinking was dominated by self-criticism and blame for failing to follow her dream of teaching high school English. Like Emily, you may have unfulfilled dreams that cause you regret. Your answers to the Domains of Regret worksheet provide the foundation for understanding the life experiences that trigger your repetitive thoughts of regret.

Another way to assess regretful thinking is to determine whether your experience meets the criteria for RNT. Many of the items in the next exercise refer to the contributors of regret (see figure 5.1).

Exercise: The Regrets Checklist

The following statements refer to various ways of experiencing regretful thought. Based on the regret experiences you wrote about in the previous exercise, circle the rating that indicates how well the statement describes your experience of regret using a five-point scale:

-2 = strongly disagree

-1 = disagree

0 = neither disagree nor agree (neutral)

+1 = agree

+2 = strongly agree

Regret Statement	Score				
1. I often experience regret for past actions and decisions.	-2	-1	0	+1	+2
2. I often think about ways I could have made better choices or taken a better course of action.	-2	-1	0	+1	+2
3. I often wish I could live parts of my life over again.	-2	-1	0	+1	+2
4. I often think about past mistakes and actions.	-2	-1	0	+1	+2
5. I often daydream about what could have been.	-2	-1	0	+1	+2
6. I frequently think to myself, *If only...*	-2	-1	0	+1	+2
7. I blame myself for poor choices I made in the past.	-2	-1	0	+1	+2
8. Often I am filled with doubt after making an important decision.	-2	-1	0	+1	+2
9. When feeling regret, I have difficulty understanding why I made such a poor choice in the past.	-2	-1	0	+1	+2
10. I often think about how much better my life could have been had I made better choices.	-2	-1	0	+1	+2
11. I often think about making changes now that would reduce the negative effects of a poor decision in the past.	-2	-1	0	+1	+2
12. Whenever I think about what could have been, it always seems so much better than my current life circumstance.	-2	-1	0	+1	+2

Item construction and response options are based on regret and repetitive thought scales developed by Roese et al. (2009).

There are no established cut-off scores because the checklist was developed for this workbook. If you summed the statement values you circled and the total score was a negative value or zero, it is unlikely you experience persistent and repetitive regretful thinking. The higher your score in the positive range, the greater the likelihood you have significant regret that is at times intense, repetitive, and distressing.

Test the Options Strategy

We've seen that regret is more intense when we focus on our past failures of inaction, believe there is a more desirable alternative, and think there is still opportunity to take corrective action to achieve the alternative. But this way of thinking can create a false hope that keeps us stuck in regret. It's important to evaluate whether this better alternative is still doable or whether there are other options available that could diminish your regretful thinking. We'll use a problem-solving strategy called "mental contrasting" to evaluate whether the desired alternative you've been thinking about is futile or not (Krott and Oettingen 2018).

Exercise: Examine My Options

This exercise provides a step-by-step method for reexamining your regret of inaction. It's important to spend time working on each step in the order it is presented. The steps are intended to lead you to accepting that it's time to abandon the desired choice that you failed to make in the past and to considering an alternative course of action that is doable at the present time.

Step 1. The Desired Alternative

Select the most frequent and distressing regret you listed in the Domains of Regret exercise. Review what you wrote in the third column as the desired decision or regrettable inaction you should have taken. Use the following questions to think more deeply about what makes this alternative decision or action more desirable to you than what actually happened.

1. What makes this desired decision or regrettable inaction a much better alternative than the choice you made?

    _____

    _____

    _____

2. How would your present life be better if you had made the alternative decision or action?

    _____

    _____

3. What would you have needed to do differently to have made this decision or taken this course of action?

    _____

    _____

4. Circle whether you have high or low expectation that you would have succeeded in producing the desired outcome.

    HIGH EXPECTATION   LOW EXPECTATION

Step 2. Current Obstacles

Think of the desired alternative as a goal that you could still pursue today. What are the obstacles that would hinder you from pursuing the desired alternative at the present time? Be specific about the obstacles that would interfere in making your wished outcome come true. Provide as much detail on the anticipated obstacles as you can. Use a blank sheet if you need more space for additional obstacles.

1. _____

2. _____

3. _____

4. _____

5. _____

Step 3. Evaluate and Consider an Alternative Outcome

In light of the obstacles listed in step 2, is it still feasible to assume there is time to pursue the desired outcome or regrettable inaction? If not, write down why it would be better to abandon this desired outcome. What are the advantages of letting go of the desired alternative decision or regrettable inaction of the past?

_____

_____

_____

Next, consider an alternative goal that might not produce the most desired outcome but would be an improvement over the current situation. The alternative should bypass or overcome most of the obstacles listed in step 2. It should be a personally significant goal that fosters high commitment and expectation of success. State the alternative goal in specific terms and then list the steps you will take to reach the goal.

My alternative goal (outcome): _____

What I need to do to reach the alternative outcome:

1. _____

2. _____

3. _____

4. _____

5. _____

Were you able to complete the three steps in this exercise? When experiencing repetitive or self-blame regret, people treat their forsaken choice or regrettable inaction of the past as something they can still correct. Listing the obstacles to corrective action in step 2 and considering a different approach to your current undesirable situation in step 3 will help shift your focus from *what I should have done* to *what I can do now to improve my situation.* If you have difficulty completing these steps, consider asking your therapist or someone close to you for assistance.

Emily had several regrets, so she'd need to complete the Examine My Options exercise for each one. For illustrative purposes, let's take her regret about quitting university in the second year of her undergraduate program in English. In the third column of the previous exercise, she wrote, *I'd like to go back, finish my English major, get my teaching certificate, and teach high school English.* To understand why this alternative course of action was so desirable, Emily might provide the following answers to the questions in step 1:

1. *Positive aspects. Completing my degree would eliminate the shame I feel about quitting university, it would boost my self-confidence, and a teaching job would provide much-needed extra income.*

2. *Better present life. I'd feel more independent, valued, and less trapped at home; no longer an underachiever.*

3. *A different past. I needed to realize that accomplishment and career success were much more important to my self-worth and life satisfaction. I also needed to be more assertive with my husband about my needs and ambitions.*

4. *Expectation. I believe I could have finished my degree and had children along with a full-time teaching job.*

In step 2 of the exercise, there are several obstacles Emily could list about returning to university and pursuing a teaching certification.

1. *Life would be extremely stressful and chaotic if I went to school given all my responsibilities at home.*

2. *My time is not flexible, so how could I attend classes that don't fit with my schedule?*

3. *School fees are costly, and money is tight.*

4. *Even if I finished, there are few teaching vacancies in my community, and I'm not free to move where there are more job opportunities.*

5. *I'm older now and would have no teaching experience. How can I compete with younger single people for these jobs?*

When Emily examined the obstacles in step 2, she realized she needed to abandon her desire to teach high school. In step 3, she came up with an alternative option that was much more feasible. It was:

I can still complete my English major by taking online courses and switching to a university that specializes in advanced education for working people. Once I've completed my degree, I'll explore the possibility of a further degree in human resources. I love interacting with people, and I've always felt like I may have a knack for business. I'm being unrealistically narrow to think that teaching high school is the only job that can give me meaning and fulfillment.

Like Emily, are you holding on to an alternative choice or a regrettable inaction that is no longer feasible? By abandoning this alternative and working on a more realistic option, you're letting go of *what I should have done.* Letting go of the should is an important part of loosening the hold of regret. Instead, focusing on *what I can do now* will give you a sense that you're moving on with your life rather than being stuck in the past with repetitive thoughts of blame and regret.

The Discrepancy-Reduction Strategy

With the passage of time, we forget why we made the choice we now regret. Previously we called this the "explanation deficit," and it's one of the reasons for repetitive regretful thinking (see figure 5.1). None of us has a perfectly accurate memory. And time only makes our memory more biased and inaccurate. Add to this the intense self-blame of regret, and it's easy to see why the reasons for a poor decision are no longer clear. We judge ourselves harshly because we see the decision from what we now know rather than from what we knew in the past (this is the hindsight bias). You may even get to the point of being totally mystified by how you could have made such a bad decision. In your regret, you might think over and over, *How could I have been so stupid?* This explanation deficit will be an important reason why you're stuck in regret. It also provides a clue for how to get yourself beyond regret.

Another problem that contributes to the explanation deficit is the discrepancy between what happened and how you like to see yourself. We all like to think of ourselves as a conscientious, intelligent, and responsible individual who makes good decisions. When a bad decision is made, this creates a discrepancy with how we like to view ourselves. If you can justify the bad decision by blaming it on factors outside your control or things unknown to you at the time, you're likely to conclude, *I made the best decision with the information I had at the time.* What you're doing is justifying your bad decision or regrettable inaction. This will reduce the discrepancy between having made a poor choice and your belief that you are a responsible, competent decision-maker. In turn, your justification will reduce feelings of regret because you come to believe you did your best with what you knew at the time. Use the next exercise to rediscover whether you might have been more justified in making a regrettable decision than you've been thinking.

Exercise: Reevaluate Your Decision Making

Part A. Regret Narrative

Select the most regrettable decision you listed on the Domains of Regret worksheet. Schedule two or three thirty-minute memory recall sessions in which you try to remember as vividly as possible the time when you made the regrettable decision or action. It is important to imagine as much detail as possible about this past experience. Your answers to the following questions will help you reconstruct your memory of the regrettable experience.

- Where were you, what were you doing, and who was with you at the time you made the regrettable decision?

  _____

  _____

- Was there anything that stood out about the situation or circumstances around the time of the regrettable decision or action? _____

  _____

- Did you discuss with anyone what you were planning to do? What advice did they give you?

  _____

  _____

- Were you fully aware of all the options available to you at that time? What were they?

  _____

  _____

- How were you feeling at the time? Did your emotional state have any influence on your decision making?

  _____

  _____

- Were there any other external factors that influenced your decision? If so, what were they?

  _____

  _____

- Was there anything else that influenced your decision or limited your freedom to choose between several options?

  _____

  _____

- Did you think of the advantages and disadvantages of your decision or action at the time? If yes, list as many as you can remember.

  _____

  _____

Next, write a brief paragraph that describes as accurately as possible what you remember about making the regrettable decision based on your answers to the previous questions. Use the space provided to record your regret narrative.

_____

_____

_____

_____

_____

_____

_____

Part B. Justification Analysis

Answer the next set of questions based on the regret narrative.

1. Did you make an informed decision or take a course of action based on the information available at the time even though you now have regrets?	Yes	No
2. Were you aware you were making a poor decision or action that you'd later regret?	Yes	No
3. Did you intentionally choose a worse option because it was easier in the short term knowing that it would cause undesirable effects later?	Yes	No
4. Do you now realize there were other factors that influenced you at the time or limited your ability to choose a better option?	Yes	No
5. Even though your past decision or action has caused regret, was it consistent with your personal values and life rules at the time?	Yes	No
6. Have you been inflating the importance of the past decision or action because of feeling regret?	Yes	No
7. Are you still a responsible, thoughtful person even though you made this regretful past decision or action?	Yes	No
8. Do you now believe you were not solely responsible for the regrettable decision or action?	Yes	No
9. Is hindsight bias evident, where you think of the regrettable decision or action because now you know a future you could not have known in the past?	Yes	No
10. Can you imagine other competent people making the same decision or action you took based on what you knew in the past?	Yes	No

If you circled no to questions 2 and 3, and yes to all the other questions, then you now realize you were more justified in making the regrettable decision than you have been thinking. Write a brief paragraph on why you now believe *I made the best decision or took the best action based on what I knew at the time.*

_____

_____

_____

_____

_____

_____

_____

People experience repetitive regretful thinking when they can't understand why they made such a poor decision or failed to act in the past. The inability to justify a past undesirable choice is an important contributor to regretful thinking. Your work on the last exercise guided you toward rediscovering the reasons why you made the regrettable decision or failed to make a better choice. These reasons are your justification for the decision-making process you took in the past given the information available to you and the circumstances at that time. Is this the conclusion you reached from the exercise? Have you come to a new understanding, a more forgiving and compassionate attitude toward yourself? If you have, your more forgiving attitude might sound like this.

> *Unfortunately, I made a poor choice in the past, and I missed a good opportunity, but I now realize I was doing the best I could at the time given the circumstances and what I knew. I'm being unfair to myself to judge my past actions and decisions based on hindsight. It's time to move on from the past, accept that the past can't be changed, and instead deal with my present difficulties in a more constructive manner.*

Emily could develop a more forgiving attitude toward quitting university by discovering a new understanding of the decision. She might recall that as university students, she and her husband were financially strapped, that she had doubts that an English major was the right choice for her, that her grades were slipping because of disinterest, and that she always knew she'd go back to school eventually. In fact, at the time, the plan was to take off just a couple of semesters, but she was lucky to find a permanent job with a good salary, and so time just slipped away. A deeper reevaluation of the reasons for quitting university would help Emily realize she was justified for making this decision. Many young women made similar decisions, and like Emily, they probably found the passage of time and changing life circumstances led to their present situation. For Emily, it was time to be more self-forgiving and move beyond her regret of the past. It was time to deal with the present and develop a new plan to further her education. Like Emily, you'll be able to move beyond your regret only when you realize you did your best in the past, but now it's time to let go of *what you should have done*. The "should've, could've" is forever gone. Better to focus on an alternative course of action that will boost positive emotion and well-being rather than continue being mired in repetitive regretful thinking.

Wrap-Up

In this chapter you learned:

- Repetitive regretful thinking is a type of rumination that involves repeated self-blame for what might have been a better outcome. It's dominated by "should've, could've" thinking that can lead to self-depreciation and contribute to negative emotional states, like depression, anxiety, and guilt.

- There are seven processes that increase the risk of falling victim to repetitive regret: (1) experiencing a significant and enduring negative outcome due to a past decision, (2) focusing on the failure to act, (3) imagining a better alternate scenario to what actually happened, (4) believing that a past bad decision can still be corrected, (5) being unable to justify the bad decision, (6) believing you were solely responsible and in control of making the decision, and (7) experiencing self-blame after making the decision.

- The Domains of Regret and Regrets Checklist are two assessment tools that can help you determine whether you're experiencing repetitive regretful thinking.

- Testing your options is a strategy that focuses on correcting the perception that a lost opportunity due to a poor choice or failure to choose a better pathway can still be realized today. It is better to redirect your efforts toward working on a different, more realistic alternative that focuses on what can be done to improve your present situation.

- Reevaluating your past decision making is a strategy that helps you rediscover the reasons for your regrettable decision or inaction of the past. Being able to justify why you made a poor choice in the past is critical to moving beyond regret. It's an effective approach for countering hindsight bias that only intensifies self-blame and regretful thinking.

What's Next?

Getting stuck in regret is a self-defeating form of RNT because the past can't be changed. Reevaluating your present options and past decision making will get you to an acceptance of the past as "what happened, happened" and encourage you to live in the moment. You'll have more self-forgiveness and compassion despite your poor choices and inaction in the past and be able to take a more problem-oriented approach to your present situation. But persistent regret is not the only negative emotion tied to the past. As you'll see in the next two chapters, past experiences can also produce two other negative emotions: shame and humiliation.

CHAPTER 6

• • • • •

Confront Shame

No doubt you've often heard it stated, "You must believe in yourself." In truth, its importance cannot be understated. Belief in one's personal worth and value is the bedrock of happiness and well-being. A healthy sense of self-worth is associated with success, satisfying relationships, and positive emotions. If you doubt your personal worth, you'll have lower life satisfaction, more negative emotions, and a greater risk of mental health problems.

This chapter focuses on repetitive negative thinking associated with shame. Shame is a socially based emotion that can have a devastating impact on self-worth. We begin by considering one of the central ingredients in shame RNT: the importance we place on what people think of us. You'll be introduced to Joan, who struggled with shame whenever she thought about her husband's infidelity. This is followed by assessment tools that you can use to determine whether you have repeated thoughts of shame about a past social interaction. The second half of the chapter presents two strategies that weaken the grip of painful thoughts of shame.

Looking to Each Other

How we think about our personal value is learned through a lifetime of social experiences. What others think of us is the most important way we determine our self-worth. This is why most of us are deeply concerned about what people think of us. We look for evidence that we are loved, accepted, and valued by people who are influential in our lives. This type of positive feedback strengthens beliefs in our self-worth. But criticism, rejection, and disapproval threaten our belief in our personal value. When this happens, repetitive negative thoughts of low self-worth and self-criticism are triggered, along with a surge of negative feelings.

Negative interactions with others can make us anxious and fearful about what other people think of us. Do you find yourself anxious in social situations, worried about your impression on others? Are you repeatedly thinking, *I wonder what they think of me? Do they like me? Am I making a good impression?* If these questions often flood your mind, low self-esteem might be causing you to expect negative judgment and disapproval whenever you meet people.

Unfortunately, our society can be quite hostile and unforgiving. Power and dominance are rampant, which increases the likelihood of distressing social experiences. In all social settings we instantly become aware of a "pecking order," which is determined by how much control, power, recognition, and influence we have over others. People higher in the pecking order have more power and prestige, whereas those at the bottom are more submissive, powerless, and isolated. Naturally, it is better to be on top, so we strive to improve our status and avoid anything that would threaten our approval and acceptance by others. This is because higher social status boosts thoughts of self-worth, whereas a reduction in social status causes us to think less of ourselves.

One of the most important indicators of status is how much attention we receive from others (Gilbert 1997). Think back to the last time you were ignored in a social gathering. How did you feel? Most people find being ignored highly distressing. It causes them to question their value, to have repetitive negative thoughts like, *I have so little value to these people they won't even acknowledge my presence.* When we're ignored, our social status has come under assault. Depending on the importance of the situation, we may end up ruminating on what happened and what it means to our self-worth. But being ignored is not the only negative social experience that reduces our social attractiveness and threatens self-worth. Shame is a more extreme social experience that can damage our social standing and destroy self-worth, respect, and dignity.

Shame: An "Unworthy" Emotion

Shame and its related emotion, humiliation, belong to a group of emotions called the *self-conscious emotions*. These emotions happen in social situations. They are concerned with keeping our relationships healthy and increasing positive attention from others. Shame is *an intense feeling of distress that includes a strong negative self-judgment ("bad, stupid me") caused by an unfavorable (embarrassing) experience or action that threatens a loss of social status and acceptance by others. There is a strong urge to hide, avoid, or escape relevant social situations.* It is often associated with making an insensitive or "stupid" comment in front of others (an audience). And when this happens, our mind can be filled with repetitive negative thinking about the shame experience.

Shame and humiliation share many qualities. They both involve (a) loss of self-esteem and status, (b) a sense of powerlessness, (c) feelings of inferiority, and (d) a sense of being treated unfairly in the presence of others (Elshout, Neilissen, and van Beest 2017). Yet, in other ways, they are different. With shame, people blame themselves for an embarrassing situation, so they end up with a negative self-evaluation. With humiliation, people believe another person is entirely responsible for their degradation, so the end result is a greater sense of powerlessness. Shame can lead to depression, guilt, and even suicidal urges, whereas humiliation more likely results in anger and a desire for revenge (Gilbert 1997). The next chapter focuses on humiliation. But first, consider the following example that describes one of the most common sources of shame: marital infidelity.

Joan's Story: Facing the Shock of Betrayal

Joan was concerned about her marriage. She had been with Eugene for twenty-two years. The first ten years were great, but with the birth of their daughters and the stresses of family life, the relationship had become strained and stale. Life was hectic, and the couple had grown apart. Eugene had become emotionally cold and distant, while Joan found herself more impatient and frustrated. It seemed like they bickered over everything. There was little intimacy in the marriage, and date nights had ceased long ago. Joan realized she was increasingly critical of Eugene, often complaining that he was not taking enough family responsibility. For his part, Eugene was spending less time at home, blaming the late nights and odd weekend away on work. He was irritable at home and showed no physical interest in Joan. He had stopped touching her months ago, which made her concerned that he no longer found her physically attractive. The sexual chemistry they once enjoyed had vanished. Joan wondered if her age and weight gain bothered Eugene who had always been concerned with physical appearance and beauty. She suggested they seek marital counseling, but Eugene refused.

As the months passed, Joan became more and more suspicious of Eugene's absences. She started checking up on him at work. She discovered that his excuses didn't add up. Finally, she went through his phone and found several intimate text messages to her best friend. She confronted Eugene, and he finally admitted to having a two-year affair with Joan's friend. This came as a devastating shock to Joan. What made it worse was that the betrayal involved her best friend and several of Joan's other girlfriends knew about it but didn't tell her. Along with the sadness and sense of loss came another emotion that surprised Joan. She felt a profound sense of shame and embarrassment. She couldn't stop thinking that so many knew of Eugene's infidelity before her. Whenever in social situations, she'd have persistent thoughts that people were thinking she was weak, naïve, and stupid. She even questioned whether they might be blaming her for driving Eugene from the marriage. She concluded that they no longer respected her, and she was now the object of pity. She could sense their judgment, and this persistent negative thinking filled her with feelings of shame. Like Joan, millions have suffered the heart-wrenching shame of intimate betrayal.

Embarrassment and Shame Experiences

Shame is embarrassment in the extreme. So, we begin with embarrassment to understand shame. Embarrassment occurs when we accidentally violate some social rule or custom and think that our reputation might be damaged. Embarrassment tends to be sudden, unexpected, but only mildly distressing. It often fades quickly and can occur in trivial, even humorous, circumstances. We can start with times of embarrassment and ask whether any of these experiences have developed into shame.

No doubt you can think of an endless number of ways you've felt embarrassed. Some examples include forgetting something you should have known, exaggerating a point, not being completely truthful, making a stupid comment or mistake, and the like. In each example, we do something that's inappropriate to the social setting, and the offense is noticed by others. So, embarrassment mainly occurs when we have an audience.

When was the last time you felt really embarrassed? Most of us try to forget these experiences because they only make us feel bad about ourselves. But embarrassment is a good starting point for work on shame because it forces you to consider whether any negative social experiences might be contributing to your emotional distress. You can use the next worksheet to list your most memorable moments of embarrassment.

Exercise: Embarrassing Experiences

Think back to times when you felt embarrassed. It may have been caused by something you said, how you acted, or being inappropriate in the situation. State what you did and how those around you reacted. Did you show your embarrassment (such as become red in the face), or did you keep it hidden? Were there any negative consequences from the embarrassment?

1.	6.
2.	7.
3.	8.
4.	9.
5.	10.

If you had difficulty recalling times of embarrassment, try thinking about what happened in different phases of your life, like high school, college or university, dating experiences, employment or career experiences, friendships, travel, leisure, and the like. Did anything go wrong where you felt embarrassed? If you are still having trouble remembering, ask someone you've known for a long time if they can remember you doing anything embarrassing. If you've been able to list several embarrassing experiences, place an asterisk beside the experiences that were most significant.

Joan could think of many times when she felt embarrassed. For example, she recalled making a comment in a work meeting that others criticized as uninformed. Her face got red, her body tensed, and her stomach churned. She thought, *I've made a fool of myself,* but the embarrassment faded quickly because she was convinced that she had a strong reputation with coworkers she'd known for years. But her emotions and repetitive thinking about the infidelity were much deeper and prolonged. They went well beyond embarrassment, although at any moment she could feel embarrassed when she encountered someone who knew about the affair.

Shame is a more intense emotion that involves a loss of social status, leaving the person feeling inferior, rejected, and excluded (Gilbert 1997). People who feel shamed want to run and hide from others. They have repetitive negative thoughts of self-criticism and perceived rejection by the audience, and so their self-worth takes a hit. People shamed keep thinking, *I'm a bad person,* and blame themselves for a social violation or not meeting the expectations of others.

Many different social situations can trigger shame. A graduate student is called stupid by his professor in front of his fellow undergraduate and graduate students. A husband criticizes his wife's weight gain during dinner with friends. A new employee arrives late to a meeting and is called out by the manager. An experienced manager's application for an executive position is turned down when everyone expected her to get the promotion. For Joan, the feeling of shame never left but only intensified when anything reminded her that Eugene had been quite public about his infidelity but for some reason, she remained oblivious to it for many months.

Many experiences can cause shame, from the fairly ordinary to very serious, traumatic incidents, like physical or sexual abuse, crimes, and infidelity. In all instances, our repetitive thinking focuses on having done something wrong, believing there is an audience that is passing judgment, and a belief that social status and self-worth have been lost. Occasionally, we feel shame for a private experience if we keep thinking how much worse it would be if others knew (Tangney et al. 1996). Also, we can feel ashamed of feelings that we judge unacceptable like, *I'm ashamed that I feel so much anger and resentment toward my ex* (Leahy 2015). Do any of these descriptions of shame sound familiar to you? The next exercise will help you begin the process of determining whether shame is a factor in your emotional distress.

Exercise: Shame Experiences

Think back to the different phases of your life and whether you've had times of shame. Review the embarrassing experiences you marked with an asterisk and consider whether these qualify as shame experiences. If any of these experiences meet the five characteristics of shame listed below, write them in the space provided.

1. The experience was highly distressing.

2. You broke a social rule (norm) or didn't meet expectations.

3. You felt a loss of social acceptance, value, and status.

4. You had thoughts of worthlessness, inferiority, or incompetence from the experience.

5. You tried to hide or avoid others in order to conceal your shame.

1. _____

2. _____

3. _____

4. _____

5. _____

If you've experienced trauma or significant hurt, you may have felt shame. You'll want to include these experiences on your worksheet. Most often, experiences of shame are easy to remember. So, if you couldn't recall any shame experiences, the shame emotion may not be relevant for you. If you listed several experiences, place an asterisk beside the one that you think about repeatedly. This is the shame experience you'll want to use when we get to the strategies section.

Embarrassment and shame are distressing emotions that spring from negative social experiences involving an audience or witnesses. Embarrassment is the milder negative feeling that we get over quickly. We either forget about it or we're able to laugh at ourselves when telling others about the experience. Embarrassment is rarely associated with RNT.

Shame is much different. It's a self-conscious emotion that can "cut to the bone," causing repeated negative thinking about self-worth and social value. The RNT of shame often focuses on themes of defeat, deflation, and inferiority to others. This way of thinking can persist for years, causing significant emotional distress.

Assessing Shame

Were some of your shame experiences not characterized by RNT and persistent distress? The fact is, not all shame is unhealthy. If you've dealt with the shame, it can have little impact on your life. But we can get stuck in our shame, and the experience becomes a major factor in our emotional distress. When shame is unhealthy, it takes on the characteristics of RNT.

Below is a checklist of various ways we can respond to shame experiences. By completing this checklist, you'll learn whether shame is a problem for you. You'll rate how you coped with the most significant shame experience listed on the previous worksheet.

Exercise: The Shame Checklist

Review your work in the Shame Experiences exercise and select the one experience that you think about repeatedly. Write that experience in the space provided. Next, use a checkmark to indicate how well each statement describes (applies to) your response to the shame experience when you think about it.

Distressing shame experience I think about most: _____

_____

When I think back to what happened...	0 Does Not Apply	1 Applies Somewhat	2 Moderately Applies	3 Very Much Applies	4 Completely Applies
1. It still upsets me.					
2. I blame myself.					
3. I feel condemned by people who know about it.					
4. I try to avoid thinking about it.					
5. The thoughts just seem to come from nowhere.					
6. I feel guilty.					
7. I think about how stupid, weak, or defective I must be.					
8. I think my reputation has been ruined.					
9. I can't stop myself thinking about the experience even though I want to.					
10. I often wish I had acted differently.					
11. I think about the bad impression I made on others.					
12. I can't talk about what happened.					

When I think back to what happened...	0 Does Not Apply	1 Applies Somewhat	2 Moderately Applies	3 Very Much Applies	4 Completely Applies
13. It feels so awful, I can practically relive the entire experience in my mind.					
14. I feel embarrassed and ashamed.					
15. I dwell on it and how badly it has affected my life.					
16. I'm concerned it's weakened my connection with friends or family.					

If most of your ratings were 2 to 4, then it's likely you're experiencing RNT shame. The higher your score, the more likely RNT shame is contributing to your personal distress. If your statement scores are in the 0 to 1 range, you've probably normalized the shame. If you are having difficulty with the Shame Checklist, your therapist or counselor can help you explore whether shame is relevant for your emotional distress.

Joan's Unhealthy Response

If Joan experienced RNT shame, she would be thinking about the betrayal almost continuously and have difficulty switching her attention to something else. Thoughts of the betrayal would be highly distressing, and she might ruminate on why it happened. She'd have RNTs of self-blame and accusation, convinced she wasn't a good wife and that's why Eugene cheated. She might dwell on all her negative qualities and come to believe she was an undeserving and undesirable person. She might feel embarrassed when reminded that others knew about the affair before her. Her thoughts would turn to how naïve and defective she looks to her friends. She might view herself as weak and pathetic, doubting whether her friends even want to associate with her. She'd increasingly avoid others and withdraw into herself to reduce feeling shame. Does this way of thinking sound familiar to you? If your responses to the Shame Checklist are consistent with Joan's, then you may be experiencing RNT shame.

Joan's Healthy Response

When thinking of the betrayal, Joan would hold Eugene responsible for breaking their marriage vows. She would think about his dishonesty, deceitfulness, and selfishness as the reasons for the betrayal rather than blame herself as a deficient partner. She wouldn't allow the betrayal to become the measure of her worth. Instead, she'd continue to believe she's a competent, compassionate, and understanding woman who had been betrayed by the man she trusted. Joan would reassert her dignity and respect with friends and family members by believing in their support and understanding. She would seek to gain a wider perspective on the betrayal by noting that, unfortunately, infidelity has become far too common in our society. Strong, successful, popular, and resilient women are also betrayed by their lovers. So rather than hide, avoid, and isolate herself, Joan would choose to face her friends and deal with the many decisions that must be made about the marriage. Because of its importance, Joan would be deep in thought about the infidelity, but she wouldn't let it become the totality of who she is.

Have you discovered that shame plays a greater role in your emotional distress than you realized? Did you list several shame experiences, or, like Joan, is there one major life event that you continually think about? Did you identify more strongly with Joan's unhealthy response to the betrayal? If you've concluded RNT shame is a problem, there is good news. You can use the following two shame reduction strategies to reduce RNT shame's negative impact in your life.

Reduction Strategy: Take a Healthier Perspective

The RNT triggered by shame experiences can feel like worry, rumination, and regret. That's why it's helpful to take a second look at these other types of RNT. Has your memory of the shame experience become more biased over time? Is it possible you're exaggerating its impact and how badly you look to others? Are you blaming yourself for what happened? Just like worry, rumination, and regret, recovery from shame depends on thinking differently about the experience. Use the following four-step exercise to change how you think about your shame experience.

Exercise: Perspective Taking

Each of the following steps focuses on a distinct aspect of shame thinking. Complete all of the steps in the order presented to gain the most from this exercise. First, write down your most distressing shame from the Shame Experiences exercise.

Distressing shame experience I think about most: _____

_____

_____

_____

_____

_____

Step 1. Consequences

Set aside thirty minutes to think deeply about the short- and long-term consequences of the distressing shame experience. In the left column, list specific, real-life evidence that the shameful experience has had a negative effect on your life. Next, use the right column to list important ways that your life has been unaffected by the shame experience. To help with your answers, imagine how a friend or family member would evaluate the impact of the shame experience on your life. Include what they might think in your lists.

Ways My Life Has Been Badly Affected by the Shame Experience	Ways My Life Has Not Been Affected by the Shame Experience
1.	1.
2.	2.
3.	3.
4.	4.
5.	5.
6.	6.
7.	7.

What do you notice from the two lists? Are you overthinking the negative effects of the shame experience? Are you surprised that important parts of your life are unaffected by the experience? Have your RNTs about the experience caused you to exaggerate its negative personal impact?

Step 2. Blame

When we experience an unfortunate social event, we'll feel shame if we blame ourselves but guilt if we blame our behavior (Tangney and Dearing 2002). Are you feeling shame when you should be feeling guilt? Was the unfortunate experience due to a flaw or deficiency in your personality, or was it due to an error or misunderstanding that was specific to a situation and your behavior? Use the following questions to think more deeply about whether it's you or your behavior to blame.

1. What are the deficiencies or weaknesses in my character that caused the shame experience?

   _____

   _____

2. What was unique about this circumstance that caused me to act in an embarrassing or unfavorable way?

   _____

   _____

Do you see the difference between (1) blaming yourself versus (2) blaming your behavior? Imagine you feel shame for making an unkind remark about a close friend in front of others. You'll feel shame if you blame yourself by thinking, *There I go again; I'm such an unkind, selfish, back-stabber.* On the other hand, if you think, *Where did that rude remark come from? I'm usually more careful with my conversation. I must have gotten carried away in the conversation.* Blame is more condemning when it focuses on a personal flaw. Shifting the blame to a mistaken action that is a specific to the situation will reduce its intensity.

Step 3. Audience

Think about who was present when you experienced the shame. RNT associated with shame often focuses on imagining that we've lost the approval, respect, and social status of valued people. We can't know what people who witnessed our shameful experience really think, so we're left guessing. The following worksheet asks that you look for specific realistic evidence that you lost the respect of others. It's important to look beyond what you imagine to what really happened at the time of the incident and afterward. In the second column, list evidence that you're still respected and valued by some individuals important in your life.

Evidence That I've Permanently Lost the Respect of Others Due to the Shame Experience	Evidence That I Still Have the Respect of Others Despite the Shame Experience
1.	1.
2.	2.
3.	3.
4.	4.
5.	5.
6.	6.
7.	7.

After doing the work in step 3, did you discover lots of evidence that you're still valued and respected by others? When shameful thinking becomes repetitive, it seems so obvious that we've lost the respect of others, that people can't see beyond the shameful incident. It's important to realize how you think of the shame is not how other people think of it. For them, it's not the defining moment, the totality of who you are. To them, you are much more than your shame!

Step 4. Alternative View

Are you beginning to see a different way to think of your shame experience from the work you've done so far? Did you discover important ways that your life has been unaffected by the shame experience? Is it possible the shame is due to a mistake or poor judgment rather than a personal flaw? Have you really lost as much social attraction and value to others as you think? Imagine that your closest friend experienced your shame experience. Based on your work in this exercise, what advice would you give your friend on how to think about their shame experience? What would be the most balanced, realistic perspective your friend should take? Write your advice in the space provided.

Advice to my friend: _____

_____

_____

_____

_____

Your advice probably included reasons why the shame experience is not as bad as your friend is thinking. Did you encourage your friend to stop self-blame and instead view the shame as an embarrassing act? Did you also provide evidence that people have not lost as much respect as your friend thinks? Now apply this same advice to you. Isn't this alternative view a more realistic, balanced way to think of the shame experience?

Did your work in this exercise lead you toward a more balanced, realistic way of thinking that reduced your feeling of shame? If so, it's important to put this new way of thinking into practice. Each time you think about the past experience and feel shame, shift your mind to the alternative view and think on it deeply. Think about the advice you would give your friend and how this applies to you. Consider all the ways in which your life is not defined by the shame experience. Realize you are not entirely to blame for what happened, that everyone has to live with embarrassment. Review the evidence you listed that other people still respect you despite what happened. When you slip into RNT shame, replace it with the alternative view. The more you do this, the more you'll believe in the alternative view. When this happens, you'll find that shifting your perspective can have a dramatic impact on shame.

If you had difficulty using this exercise, consider the alternative view that Joan could develop about the betrayal. Beginning with step 1, Joan could think about the women she knew who've endured a similar experience and how their lives eventually returned to normal. From her consequences list, she'd realize that the negative impact of the betrayal was more intense in the short term. It did create family and relationship problems that could last for years. But there were also important areas of her life that were relatively unaffected by the infidelity, such as the potential for career advancement, the love and support of her parents and siblings, her close relationship with her children, and the friends who rallied around her during this difficult time. She also had her health, financial stability, her faith community, and the continued opportunity to participate in recreational and leisure activities. As Joan thought more about the effects of the betrayal, she was reminded of all the ways her daily life continued as if nothing had changed.

Her work on step 2 would bring her to the realization that it was not she who changed. Rather, it was Eugene and his dishonesty, selfishness, and irresponsibility that threatened their marriage. From her work on step 3, Joan would be able to list all the evidence that others still considered her an intelligent, resourceful, and strong individual. With the passage of time, people stopped asking how she was doing and seemed to forget about Eugene's betrayal. Joan could see that extramarital affairs are so common that her friends and coworkers were much less judgmental than she expected. All of this brought Joan to a different perspective on Eugene's betrayal in step 4. Her advice to a friend (and ultimately herself) was:

> *It was Eugene who abandoned me and our children. Many couples have marital problems where the husband doesn't choose infidelity. That was Eugene's choice, and now he must take responsibility for his decision. His betrayal has shaken my life and caused much damage, but I will not let it become the defining moment for me. There are many areas of my life that continue quite unaffected by the betrayal. My work, for example, has not changed because I've been betrayed. People will blame Eugene because he's the one who cheated. I'm not that different from the woman he married. Our circumstances are stressful but not that unusual for our age group. There's lots of evidence that my friends, family, and coworkers still see me as strong and resourceful, maybe even more so after the betrayal. It is Eugene, not me, who deserves the shame. I refuse to carry his shame any longer. Instead, I'll live my daily life with strength and determination.*

Reduction Strategy: Shake the Shame

Shame is strengthened or weakened by our actions. There is a strong connection between thoughts, feelings, and behavior. For thousands of years, actors have known they can create a feeling by the way they act. And psychologists have long recognized that each emotion is characterized by a certain behavioral pattern. Shame is typically associated with an urge to hide from others (Leahy 2015).

Shortly after discovering Eugene's infidelity, Joan actively withdrew from her close friends. She avoided most social activities and any chitchat with coworkers. Shame even changed Joan's demeanor. When forced to interact with people, she was quieter, less spontaneous, avoided eye contact, and was easily irritated. The shame of the infidelity had changed Joan, but not for the better. The desire to avoid feeling shame was now dominating her daily life. Like Joan, have you become more withdrawn and isolated due to shame?

Just like avoidance and passivity can increase shame feelings, there are other ways of behaving that can reduce repetitive thoughts and feelings of shame. If you behave in a way that is inconsistent with your current emotion, it can have an influence on how you feel. For example, encouraging people who are depressed to engage in activities that involve some enjoyment or sense of accomplishment can help lift the depression. The next series of exercises focus on discovering which behaviors you might change to reduce shame. Let's begin by identifying specific behaviors that might be contributing to RNT shame.

Exercise: Your Shame Behavior Profile

Below you'll find a list of typical ways that people respond when feeling shame. Some of these responses are attempts to cope with shame, and others deal with how people express shame. Place a checkmark beside the responses that are most relevant to your significant shame experiences.

☐ Avoid people who were present or know about the shame experience	☐ Feel tense, fidgety, keyed up
☐ Avoid places that remind me of the shame experience	☐ Feel irritated or angry
☐ Refuse to talk about the experience	☐ Get distracted or focused on my feelings
☐ Be more socially isolated and withdrawn	☐ Try hard to conceal my shame
☐ Avoid direct eye contact with people	☐ Sometimes freeze when around people who know about the experience
☐ Adopt the shame posture around people, characterized by downward gaze, slumped and rounded shoulders, and limp muscles	☐ Get red in the face or blush easily when around people who know about the experience
☐ Speak more quietly with longer pauses	☐ Feel "small" around others

Did you check at least two or three responses that typically occur because of shame? Possibly some of these are automatic physical reactions, like blushing or adopting the shame posture when around people. Others may be more intentional behaviors, like avoiding people or refusing to talk about the shame experience. If you're not sure about your shame reactions, keep a shame diary to write down your reactions. This may help you identify your shame behavior profile.

Joan would find the avoidance items most relevant. She avoided people and places that reminded her of Eugene's affair because shame was most intense in those situations. But shame also changed how she interacted with people. She was tense, curt, and distracted in her conversations. She was more passive and distant with people. Through her behavior, Joan was giving a strong message: *Leave me alone to drown in my misery*. In reality, Joan was trying to avoid feeling shame, which is one of the most disturbing of the negative emotions.

Motivation is an important ingredient when trying to change behavior. You'll need to be convinced that your current shame reactions are a problem. In most cases, this involves trying to hide or conceal from others so they can't see your shame. The next exercise examines the personal costs of this shame-related avoidance and whether it's time to make a change.

Exercise: Taking Stock of the Costs

Keep a shame diary for as long as it takes to collect several instances of feeling shame. Write in your diary how the shame and your response to it are having a negative effect on your daily life, how you function, and how you think and feel about yourself and others. Then use your diary entries to list the immediate and long-term harm caused by your shame reactions. Use a blank sheet if you need more space.

Immediate personal costs of my shame reactions:

1. _____

2. _____

3. _____

4. _____

5. _____

Long-term personal costs of my shame reactions:

1. _____

2. _____

3. _____

4. _____

5. _____

Did you list several important costs associated with your shame reactions? If you had difficulty with this exercise, ask someone who knows you well how they think you've changed because of feeling shame. If you are seeing a therapist, this question could be explored in a therapy session. Whether you complete this exercise on your own or with assistance, it is important that you truly appreciate the importance of changing your approach to shame.

Joan could list several negative effects of her shame responses. She was losing friends because she kept turning down their invitations. She was spending a lot of time alone, ruminating on Eugene's betrayal. This was making her feel more depressed. Her coworkers had stopped chit-chatting because she was giving the message that she wanted to be left alone. She was more irritated and short-tempered with her children, and she was letting household responsibilities slide. It was clear she needed to change her approach to the affair before it completely overshadowed her life.

If you're now convinced you need to change how you cope with your shame thoughts and feelings, the next exercise will guide you through this process. At the most basic level, it involves acting as if you are not ashamed even if this is the way you feel on the inside.

Exercise: The Nonshameful Way

Look back on the responses you checked on Your Shame Behavior Profile. Each of these items represents an unhealthy shame reaction. Consider how you could turn that reaction around so you're behaving in a healthier manner. The following list provides some ideas of how you might react differently to each of the items in the Your Shame Behavior Profile.

☐ Expose myself to people who were present or know about the shame experience	☐ Tense and release specific muscles, and practice controlled breathing when beginning to feel tense
☐ Go to places that remind me of the shame experience	☐ Listen and be patient and understanding when in conversation with others
☐ Talk about the experience to trusted family, close friends, and therapist	☐ Gently bring my attention back to an external focus
☐ Force myself to be more socially engaged	☐ Be more authentic and resist efforts to conceal shame
☐ Look people in the eye when talking to them	☐ Focus on more active engagement when conversing with others
☐ Practice adopting an upright posture even when it feels unnatural	☐ Accept blushing as an automatic physiological response
☐ Be more forthright when speaking to others	☐ Accentuate myself when in social situations, such as not shying away from the attention of others

Next, write specific instructions on how you could react to your shame feelings in a healthier manner. The instructions should be unique to your situation and how you act when feeling shame. They should focus on the two or three shame responses you highlighted in Your Shame Behavior Profile. The healthy response will be the reverse of the shame reaction. It'll involve some form of engagement with people and situations despite feeling shame. If you are having difficulty creating a healthy behavior protocol, seek help from your therapist or someone close to you who knows about your struggle with shame.

My healthy shame reactions: _____

_____

_____

If you were able to write a description of how to act in a nonshameful way, it's time to put it into practice. You might want to start by practicing these healthy responses with a confidante, your partner, or therapist before employing them in real-life shame situations. We call this role-playing, and it's an old strategy used to help people learn new ways of behaving. You'll be acting as if you have no shame feelings even though you do. Start by practicing these healthy actions in nonshame situations to build up your skill. Then you can use them with the situations and people who trigger your shame. Over time, these healthy responses will become more natural. When this happens, you're likely to notice a reduction in repetitive thoughts and feelings of shame.

There are several behavioral changes Joan could make. She was avoiding close friends who knew of Eugene's affair before her. A healthier response was to start engaging with them in past activities they used to enjoy together. Joan was avoiding the gym because she and Eugene used to be members. She wanted to rejoin the same gym where she knew the staff and liked the programs. Why would she allow Eugene to drive her from the gym? Let him find another place to work out. She got back to doing lunch and coffee breaks with her coworkers and taking the initiative to ask them about their day. She worked on making eye contact, keeping her head up, and asking them about their lives. She tried to take more initiative in casual conversation and concentrated on improving her listening skills. In all this, Joan was taking control and countering her tendency to avoid with more "approach" behavior. Eventually, her changed behavior would pay dividends, and she would experience a reduction in repetitive thoughts and feelings of shame.

Confronting your shame with healthier reactions is difficult. It will take time, patience, and practice. The greater your intolerance of feeling shame, the longer it will take to break the avoidance pattern. One of the greatest challenges we face is switching from avoidance to approach because approach behavior initially causes a rise in negative emotions like shame. But together with perspective taking, adopting healthier responses to your shame is effective in shaking up repetitive shame thoughts and feelings.

Wrap-Up

In this chapter you learned:

- Shame is an intense negative emotion that involves self-blame for an embarrassing action or comment made in front of others in which individuals think they have lost the social acceptance or respect of others. It's associated with a strong urge to hide, avoid, or escape situations that might trigger feelings of shame.

- When shame takes the form of repetitive negative thoughts, belief in our worth plummets and personal distress intensifies.

- Shame is embarrassment on steroids. When feeling shame, self-blame runs rampant, and we're convinced we've lost the respect and acceptance of others. We may even experience a sense of disgrace that fuels an urge to avoid, escape, or hide from others.

- Since shame is a common negative emotion, it is important to know when your shame has taken on the RNT properties that feed personal distress.

- Reducing the distress of RNT shame is possible when inaccurate and exaggerated thinking about the cause and consequence of the shame experience are corrected and a more realistic, balanced perspective on the experience is adopted.

- Genuine reduction in shame requires behavioral change. This happens when avoidance and concealment are replaced by healthier responses that involve direct exposure to shame and its triggers.

What's Next?

Shame is not the only negative emotion linked to negative social situations. Humiliation is another self-conscious emotion that is very similar to shame. Like shame, it cuts deep and can be an important source of personal distress and withdrawal from others. But the effects of humiliation, how people cope with it, and the strategies for overcoming this debilitating experience are different from shame. This is our topic in the next chapter.

CHAPTER 7

•   •   •   •   •

Overcome Humiliation

After the liberation of France from Nazi occupation, thousands of young French women accused of sexual and romantic collaboration with German soldiers were subjected to public head-shaving and paraded through streets lined with jeering crowds. Some were half-naked, spattered with tar, and painted with swastikas. The intent was to utterly humiliate a vulnerable group that became an outlet for French anger over years of Nazi brutality.

For centuries, humiliation has played a central role in torture. The intent is to cause a psychological crisis, stripping the individual of human dignity and value (Luban 2009). The effect of extreme humiliation goes well beyond pain and suffering. Its objective is degradation—to obliterate victims' self-worth to instill a sense of being less than human.

Most people have not experienced torture or been forced to march through streets filled with taunting crowds. You may be wondering whether this chapter has any relevance to your personal distress. Unfortunately, humiliation is much more common than you may think. Every day, thousands of people are subjected to humiliating experiences that can leave deep scars on self-worth.

Think for a moment about times when you, your friends, or family experienced ridicule, scorn, contempt, bullying, put-downs, or other forms of demeaning behavior by others. This may have occurred at work, school, home, or another social situation. When these experiences happen, humiliation is a common result. Humiliation is a deeply troubling emotion that is not only intensely distressing but also attacks the very core of personal dignity and value. The humiliating experience is most often unforgettable and may be seen as a defining experience in one's life. This makes it a prime candidate for repetitive negative thinking. When we repeatedly think about our past experiences of belittlement, the feelings of humiliation can fester for months and even years. This can create a cauldron of negative thought and feelings that cause individuals to question their personal dignity, respect, and value.

This is a chapter on humiliation. We begin with an explanation of the basic features of humiliation, an emotional state not well known for most people. Next, we consider Martin, who endured years of workplace bullying. This is followed by two assessment tools for determining whether humiliation could be a contributor to your personal distress. The chapter concludes with two strategies that can rebuild self-respect and dignity in the aftermath of a humiliating experience.

The Humiliation Emotion

Humiliation is *a traumatic emotional experience involving loss of social status, rejection, or exclusion because of unpredicted, and normally undeserved, scorn, contempt, ridicule, bullying, or degradation inflicted by individuals with higher standing, influence, or authority.* The humiliator is a person in power and with authority over the victim who carries out his or her ridicule or put-downs in front of others (Hartling and Luchetta 1999). Like shame, the presence of witnesses intensifies the humiliating experience. Victims of humiliation believe the disparagement is unjust and that the humiliator is entirely responsible for creating the traumatic experience (Elshout et al. 2017).

With humiliation, we're more likely to be bullied or belittled because of who we are rather than for what we did. You may be teased or ridiculed by a coworker who's taken an "instant dislike" to you despite anything you've done. There is nothing accidental about humiliation. Humiliators know what they are doing. They want to strip the victim of his or her self-respect and inflict emotional pain and suffering. This is usually done in front of others so the victim also feels shamed.

Victims of humiliation believe they don't deserve the ridicule, but they are powerless to stop it or defend themselves (Gilbert 1997). This can result in feelings of anger and a desire for revenge. Humiliation is implicated in various mental health problems like depression, suicide, and vindictive tendencies (Elshout et al. 2017). The negative effects of humiliation are amplified by its social context. Victims believe their deficiencies have been exposed and their value diminished before others (Klein 1991). Humiliation has a cumulative effect. The longer and more numerous the humiliation experiences, the greater its negative impact. Repetitive negative thoughts about the experience, why it happened, how it affected you, and how it has become a defining life experience intensify its adverse effects. Repeated fantasies of revenge against the humiliator can also fuel the feeling of humiliation.

One in four American women and one in nine men experience intimate partner physical violence at some point in their life (National Coalition Against Domestic Violence 2019). This makes our intimate relationships one of the most common sources of humiliation. It is the emotional abuse that occurs almost universally in domestic violence that is most responsible for inflicting humiliation. A barrage of insults, cursing, threats, yelling, excessive monitoring and control, degrading remarks, and the like can have a devastating impact on a person's self-worth and contribute to mental health problems.

The toxic effects of physical and emotional abuse are due, in part, to humiliation (Negrao et al. 2005). Its impact is most devastating if the insults and derision occur in front of children, family, friends, or in public places. If you've been the victim of an abusive parent or intimate partner, humiliation may be an important part of the lingering effects of abuse. You'll find the exercises and worksheets in this chapter helpful in your efforts to overcome abuse-related humiliation.

Over 60 million American workers are victims of workplace bullying (Workplace Bullying Institute 2017). It's defined as "any repeated harmful abusive conduct that is threatening, intimidating, humiliating, work sabotage, or verbal abuse" (WBI 2017, 1). Humiliation is a common factor in workplace bullying. Most of us work alongside others in offices, stores, and factories. We answer to an authority figure, like a supervisor, manager, director, or vice president. This makes the workplace, like the home, a fertile environment for humiliation. Take, for example, the repeated humiliation Martin experienced at work.

Martin's Story: Humiliated at Work

For eleven years Martin was a claims adjustor for a large insurance company. His work involved meeting with clients to inspect property loss or damage and then filing a report that recommended compensation the insurer should pay clients. Considerable research was required, and the adjustor's report was closely evaluated by managers who were motivated to approve the lowest possible payout. Weekly group meetings involving several adjustors were common as well as daily one-on-one interactions between the adjustor and their immediate manager.

Three years ago, a new manager appointed to oversee Martin's division took an instant dislike to him. At group meetings he was loud, angry, and insulting whenever he commented on Martin's reports. He was hypercritical of Martin's reports while expressing little criticism of the other adjustors. He'd make insulting comments like, "I can't believe you haven't been fired yet," "How could you be so stupid?" or "How long have you been an adjustor?" He had a degrading nickname for Martin, who was a short, balding man with pasty white skin.

He'd ridicule, tease, and make jokes at Martin's expense, most often in front of others in order to get a laugh. He'd give Martin the more difficult cases and then impose unrealistic deadlines. Martin was a soft-spoken, reserved individual. When he occasionally spoke up at meetings, the manager would interrupt, berate, or outright ignore his comments.

The months of workplace bullying began to take a toll on Martin's physical and mental health. He was becoming more and more stressed, anxious, and fearful at work. He developed sleep difficulties and became more withdrawn. He was losing confidence in his work skills, which caused him to make more mistakes. He developed feelings of inadequacy and began to feel depressed. He developed intense stomach pains, nausea, and diarrhea, which his doctor diagnosed as irritable bowel syndrome (IBS). Most of all, Martin noticed he was feeling beaten down and thinking he was unworthy and inferior to others. He believed he lost the respect of others, who now saw him as weak and vulnerable.

Martin tried to stop the bullying. He tried to confront his manager and defend himself, but he was simply ignored or shouted down. He went to the human resources department and complained, but little was done. He then filed a formal grievance for workplace harassment. An investigation was done, the manager was reprimanded, but nothing changed. The bullying continued. Finally, Martin left, taking another job for less pay and fewer benefits.

But Martin could not escape the lingering effects of humiliation. The bullying had changed him. Self-doubt replaced self-confidence, and he could not shake the feeling that he was not as good as others. He did not deserve such treatment, and yet no one stopped it. His torment was allowed to continue. He found it hard to trust others, feeling bitter, betrayed, and victimized by a cruel and hostile world.

Like Martin, your experience with humiliation may be rooted in workplace bullying. Or you may be trapped in an abusive intimate relationship where you are subjected to withering criticism, put-downs, and insults. Possibly you can't stop thinking about an experience of biting criticism that you endured in front of others that left you feeling utterly destroyed. Maybe your most significant humiliation reaches back to your childhood or adolescence when a parent, teacher, or friend cut you to pieces, leaving you with a profound loss of value, dignity, and self-respect.

Life provides so many opportunities to experience humiliation. A middle-aged wife was sexually and physically abused by a husband who forced her to perform degrading sexual acts with others. A soldier with strong religious values was taunted and teased by his peers and superiors because of his rigid, moralistic way of living. A young man on the autism spectrum was so badly teased, bullied, and harassed at his warehouse job that he quit. A teenager was a victim of cyberbullying when she found degrading pictures, false rumors, threats, and embarrassing personal information shared on social media. A college athlete went through a hazing ritual that crossed the line, causing an unforgettable assault on dignity and self-respect.

Do any of these experiences sound familiar to you? Have you been the victim of a humiliating experience? We've all had difficult experiences with people who criticized, belittled, or teased. No doubt you felt embarrassed, maybe even shamed, and possibly it bothered you so much that you couldn't stop thinking about it for days or even weeks later. But was it a humiliating experience? If so, was the humiliation so significant that it contributes to the personal distress you now experience? The next section explains how you can assess whether your negative social experiences qualify as humiliation.

Humiliation Assessment

Occasionally mistreatment is unintended, but more often it is done by mean and insecure individuals who feel exalted by demeaning others. Hostility, anger, selfishness, and cruelty abound in our relationships. This often occurs with those we love and hold most dear. Also, mistreatment frequently involves people who have some authority or significant influence, like spouses, parents, older siblings, an admired friend, a boss, or a teacher. When determining whether humiliation plays any role in your personal distress, start by looking at important relationships. The following exercise will help you discover whether humiliation plays a part in your past social experiences.

Exercise: The Humiliating Experiences Worksheet

List past mistreatment where you were ridiculed, mocked, bullied, put down, or belittled in front of others. Briefly describe this experience by including what was done to you, who was present, who humiliated you and for how long, and how it made you feel. Mark with an *H* each experience that qualifies as humiliation according to the following criteria:

- The person(s) mistreating you had authority, power, or status over you.

- The mistreatment was unexpected, sudden, and undeserved.

- You had little responsibility or blame for triggering the mistreatment. The mistreatment was caused by *who you are* rather than by what you did.

- At least one other person was present to witness the mistreatment.

- You felt degraded, devalued, weak, and powerless.

1.	6.
2.	7.
3.	8.
4.	9.
5.	10.

Humiliation is not simply mistreatment by someone with authority or influence. It also includes its personal impact and your efforts to cope. The next exercise presents a checklist of negative consequences and coping responses often associated with mistreatment. This checklist is useful for determining whether the lingering effects of humiliation are caused by repetitive negative thoughts of the past mistreatment.

Exercise: The Humiliation Checklist

Review the humiliation experiences you listed above and select the one you continue to think about the most. Write that experience in the space provided. Next, use a checkmark to indicate how well each checklist statement describes (applies to) your response to thinking about the humiliation experience.

Distressing humiliation experience I think about most: _____

_____

_____

When I think back to what happened...	0 Does Not Apply	1 Applies Somewhat	2 Moderately Applies	3 Very Much Applies	4 Completely Applies
1. I feel angry.					
2. I think about how I was "put down" or made to feel insignificant.					
3. I can reexperience the sense of powerlessness.					
4. I often imagine getting revenge on the person who humiliated me.					
5. Memories of the experience just pop into my mind for no reason.					
6. It makes me feel down, depressed.					
7. I think about the ridicule, bullying, and scorn I was made to feel.					
8. I try hard not to think about it.					
9. I think about how unfairly I was treated because of who I am rather than what I did.					
10. I think about how I was brought down low, dishonored in front of others.					
11. I think about the damage it's done to my self-esteem.					
12. I think about how my personal boundaries were violated by a person with influence or authority over me.					
13. I can relive the humiliation so vividly.					

If most of your ratings ranged between 2 and 4, then repetitive negative thinking might be contributing to your persistent feeling of humiliation. Scores in the 0 to 1 range suggest you've normalized the humiliation. Once again, consider the help of your therapist or counselor if you had difficulty completing the checklist.

Let's take Martin's experience with workplace bullying to better understand the difference between a healthy and an unhealthy response to humiliation. After finding a new job, Martin could come to terms with the past mistreatment and returned to a healthy level of self-worth and dignity. Or repeated thoughts and memories of the manager's mistreatment could linger for months or even years. We could call this "RNT humiliation." This type of humiliation is more destructive, causing Martin to remain devalued, depressed, and discouraged.

Example of RNT Humiliation

Martin's responses to the Humiliation Checklist would indicate that he continues to have intrusive memories of his tormenting manager. The humiliation memories would be repetitive and problematic if he thought about how degraded he felt in front of others. Thinking about the powerlessness he experienced and wondering if he brought this on himself would make the memories worse. Focusing on his anger and desire for revenge against his humiliator would fuel the feeling of humiliation. Also, efforts to suppress the humiliation memories or triggers that reminded him of the manager would fan the flames of humiliation.

Example of Healthy Humiliation Response

If you've been victimized, you may have difficulty imagining a healthy way to deal with humiliation. The challenge is to move beyond the humiliation so it doesn't become the defining experience in your life. If Martin had recovered from the mistreatment, his Humiliation Checklist responses would indicate that he had downgraded the significance of the ridicule, criticism, and bullying. He would attribute the harassment to that job and his manager's flawed character rather than a defect or weakness in his self-identity. He'd realize that his coworkers would lose more respect for the manager (the humiliator) than for him. Martin would refuse to let the humiliation influence his actions or decisions, and he would face those who witnessed the workplace bullying. He would relinquish any notion of revenge because this would change nothing. In the end, he would focus on experiences that affirm his power, acceptance, and influence with the significant people in his life.

Take a moment to review your entries in the last two exercises. Which scenario do they match? Are your responses more like Martin's healthy response to humiliation, or are they more like the example of RNT humiliation? If your assessment indicates the presence of RNT humiliation, the following self-compassion and self-worth exercises will help you dial-down humiliation and regain a sense of self-respect and dignity.

First Things First: Stop the Humiliation

This chapter focuses on the lingering effects of humiliation. The exercises address repetitive negative thinking about past mistreatment that causes persistent feelings of humiliation and distress. It's assumed the abuse or mistreatment has stopped.

If you are continuing to experience ridicule, insults, bullying, or physical or emotional abuse, it's important that you discover a way to stop it. This may involve reporting the mistreatment so that action can be taken against the humiliator. Sometimes the abuse stops when it's acknowledged, monitored, and clearly not tolerated. In other cases, you may have to leave or terminate a relationship to prevent further exposure to humiliation. Martin tried to seek justice and stop the mistreatment through a formal grievance process, but it was unsuccessful. So, he ended up quitting his job and seeking other employment. Whatever course of action is necessary, it's important to stop the abuse or mistreatment. You cannot work on restoring your self-dignity as long as you are being humiliated. That's why the following exercises are intended for people who are working on regaining their dignity and self-worth after leaving an abusive or bullying relationship.

Humiliation Reduction: Self-Compassion

If you've experienced humiliation, you know it's cruel and demeaning. No doubt you're acutely aware of its short-term effect on your emotions and self-esteem, but its long-term consequences may be less obvious. An experience of humiliation makes it much harder to be kind, gracious, and compassionate toward yourself. We tend to internalize the experience, so we no longer believe we deserve love, acceptance, and respect. When this happens, negativity, self-criticism, and self-abasement replace a gentle, compassionate attitude toward one's self. For this reason, self-compassion is a critical element in healing and recovery from humiliation.

British psychologist Paul Gilbert (2009), founder of *compassion-focused therapy* (CFT), considers compassion a basic quality that is hardwired into the human brain. He defines compassion as "the attitude of lovingkindness involving a deep awareness of suffering coupled with a strong desire to relieve it." Gilbert contends that negative emotional states, like depression, anger, shame, guilt, and disappointment, are rooted in self-criticism and the experience of being devalued by others. The remedy is to strengthen self-compassion through the practice of compassionate mind-training exercises.

CFT researchers have identified six attributes of self-compassion, which are presented in the next exercise (Gilbert 2009; see also Neff 2011). Use the checklist to determine which aspects of self-compassion may need greater focus when learning to be kinder and more forgiving of yourself.

Exercise: The Self-Compassion Checklist

Below are descriptions of the six attributes of self-compassion. Place a checkmark to indicate whether a self-compassion attribute has been negatively affected by your humiliation experience(s).

Self-Compassion Attributes	Not Affected by Humiliation Experience(s)	Affected by Humiliation Experience(s)
Care for well-being: your motivation to be more caring toward yourself		
Sensitivity: your level of awareness and sensitivity of personal needs and feelings		
Sympathy: an openness and ability to be affected by your feelings, needs, and distress (this is the opposite of being hard and uncaring toward yourself)		
Distress tolerance: an ability to confront and tolerate your negative feelings, thoughts, and situations		
Empathy: your ability to understand why you think and feel the way you do		
Nonjudgment: your ability to take an accepting, noncondemning attitude toward yourself even though you've been humiliated		

The six attributes are based on P. Gilbert, The Compassionate Mind, *Oakland, CA: New Harbinger Publications, 2009, p. 209.*

Humiliation makes it difficult to practice self-compassion. The Self-Compassion Checklist can guide you in identifying which aspects of self-compassion have been most affected by your humiliation experiences. You'll want to concentrate on those attributes when you do self-compassion training. Martin, for example, might have difficulty expressing self-compassion because the workplace bullying had a particularly negative effect on distress tolerance, empathy, and nonjudgment. It was clear that Martin needed to focus on accepting that the humiliation took place because of his manager's character flaws rather than blaming himself as the victim. Which aspects of self-compassion were affected by your experiences of humiliation? What do you need to work on to boost your self-compassion?

The next step in self-compassion training has two parts. First, you'll need to confront the humiliation experience(s) so you can strengthen distress tolerance, empathy, and nonjudgment. This is done by repeatedly reliving the humiliation experience(s) in your mind. This is like the worry exposure exercise you did in chapter 3, only this time you are imagining past experiences of humiliation. This may seem like a terrible idea because the last thing you want to do is relive those awful experiences. There are five reasons why forcing yourself to repeatedly imagine the humiliation can lead to self-compassion:

- Your ability to tolerate the negative feelings associated with the memory of being humiliated will be strengthened (*distress tolerance*).

- You'll gain greater understanding of why you felt so much distress and loss of self-respect (*empathy*).

- It'll improve your awareness and openness to your feelings and the needs associated with the humiliation (*sensitivity and sympathy*).

- You'll develop a more powerful lovingkindness image, which is the second part of compassion-focused training.

- Repeatedly imagining the humiliation eventually will deaden its emotional impact.

Exercise: Humiliation Imagery

Based on the humiliation experience(s) you listed in the first exercise, write out an expanded, more detailed description of the humiliation episode in the space provided. If you had many humiliating experiences over an extended period, choose two or three incidents that are typical of what you experienced. Use the following statements as a guide to develop a more detailed humiliation narrative.

1. Describe the place or circumstance where the humiliation occurred.

2. Write down the exact words or phrases your humiliator used that were especially demeaning, insulting, or hurtful.

3. Include any physical acts of aggression, degrading acts, belittling gestures, or other behavior that disrespected you.

4. Include the names of people who witnessed the humiliation, their reaction, and what you think they were thinking and feeling.

5. Use specific emotion words to capture how you felt at the time of the humiliation and shortly afterward.

6. Include in your narrative specific thoughts you had at the time. Did you have self-critical, self-blaming, and self-loathing thoughts? Were you thinking about the meanness and injustice you were experiencing? Were you thinking of being inferior or less worthy than others?

Humiliation narrative: _____

_____

_____

_____

_____

_____

_____

After you've created the humiliation narrative, set aside twenty to thirty minutes each day to relive in your mind the humiliation experience(s). Use the narrative to form an accurate and vivid memory of the humiliation. At first you may feel intense distress when imagining the humiliation, but with time, the distress will subside. You may remember new details about the humiliation when you practice the exercise, so you'll need to revise the humiliation narrative to include this new information.

Consider the following humiliation narrative that Martin could use as part of his self-compassion training.

I can still picture the conference room where we met for weekly review meetings. All the adjustors sat around a table with Tom (the bullying manger) seated at the head. I tried to sit as far from him as possible, but he was a loud and angry person, so I always felt trapped. He seemed to glare at me, and I could feel his disdain for me as soon as he walked in. He always started the meeting with a bald joke that made me feel conspicuous because I was the only bald man at the table. He asked everyone about their workweek but me. He called me "Mr. Brown" but referred to everyone else by their first name. He was constantly interrupting me when I made my report, saying, "Mr. Brown, could you please get to the point; I don't have all day." His criticism was especially withering. I remember comments like, "I totally disagree with your conclusion," "You haven't done enough research," or "It's obvious you don't know what you're talking about." I recall how others looked down, searched their phones, and squirmed in their seats while he ridiculed me. A couple of my close friends came to me afterward and said, "Marty, you don't have to take this. You need to stand up for yourself." But it all filled me with shame, and I became increasingly anxious about those weekly meetings. On a couple of occasions, I had a panic attack and had to suddenly leave the room. I recall having to return a few minutes later to the stares of my coworkers and a sarcastic remark by Tom. I became convinced that I was no good, that I was incompetent and unable to do a job I had once done so professionally.

You're using the humiliation imagery exercise to confront a memory and feelings that already exist in your own mind. It will strengthen your distress tolerance, empathy, and understanding. If your distress doesn't decrease after ten to twelve repetitions of humiliation imagery, stop the exercise and work with your therapist to improve your response. A negative experience with the imagery exercise may be an indication that you should see a mental health professional about your humiliation experiences.

Once you've practiced confronting your memory of humiliation, it is time to turn humiliation on its head. No doubt the humiliator played a prominent role in your narrative. Now it's time to rewrite the narrative in which you imagine a compassionate person challenging the humiliator. The compassionate person is someone who provides intense love, care, understanding, and compassion toward you, the victim of humiliation. The following exercise explains how you can build self-compassion around your humiliation experience(s).

Exercise: Compassionate Imagery

Recall a parent, sibling, grandparent, close friend, mentor, teacher, or anyone who has showed compassion toward you. Think of this person's characteristics, like wisdom, inner strength, love, joy, and optimism. Recall how this compassionate person expressed warmth, caring, kindness, acceptance, understanding, and affirmation toward you. Write a detailed description of your compassionate person and specific ways in which this person expressed lovingkindness toward you.

Compassionate person: _____

_____

_____

_____

_____

_____

Next, imagine that your compassionate person was present when you were experiencing the humiliation described in the previous narrative. What would your compassionate person do if they were present during the humiliation experience? How would they respond to your humiliator? How would the compassionate person express lovingkindness toward you? Write out a compassionate scenario in the space below using the following questions as a guide.

1. What would the compassionate person say to you to counter the ridicule and insults of the humiliator?

2. How might the compassionate person show love and acceptance toward you (hold you, comfort you, and so on)?

3. What would the compassionate person say to those who witnessed the humiliation and showed support for you?

4. What would the compassionate person say to bolster your self-worth, value, dignity, and respect?

5. Recall how it feels to have the warmth, love, and understanding of the compassionate person. Imagine that you are being held in the arms of the compassionate person during the humiliation.

My compassionate narrative: _____

_____

_____

_____

_____

_____

_____

After writing an imagined compassion narrative, set aside twenty to thirty minutes each day to practice imagining the compassionate person present during the humiliation. You may find this exercise a little more difficult because you are inventing a new image rather than reliving something that happened. At first, you may not feel comforted by the compassionate imagery, but with repetition, you'll find your attention shifting away from hurt and self-criticism toward love and acceptance. This will become the basis for practicing greater self-compassion whenever you are reminded of the humiliation you experienced.

The following is an example of Martin's self-compassion narrative to the workplace bullying.

Since my earliest childhood, my grandfather showed me unconditional love and acceptance. I can imagine him sitting beside me during those terrible weekly meetings. He was a towering figure—strong and self-assured. If he were present, he'd confront Tom for his insulting remarks. He'd insist that he treat me in a professional manner and remind Tom of my competence and conscientiousness. He'd put his arm around me and speak to the anger, bitterness, and insecurity of Tom, the little man who was threatened by my very presence. My grandfather would remind me how much I am loved and the many ways I'm admired by family and friends. I can feel the warmth and love of my grandfather, the confidence he has in me, and his belief in my value and goodness. Because my grandfather was the strong patriarch in our extended family, it is his view of me that is most authentic because he knows me so deeply from birth until now. It is his voice and his lovingkindness that I wrap around me in this hour of need.

We instinctively know that the compassion and support of others is needed in the face of trauma, abuse, or humiliation. It is more difficult to understand that we also need self-compassion. Blame, criticism, resentment, and bitterness do not restore dignity and self-worth. Rather, it's the practice of love, kindness, acceptance, and understanding that promotes healing and wholeness. The exercises in this section can bolster an attitude of self-compassion, but there is more you can do to overcome the ill effects of humiliation.

Humiliation Reduction: The Good in Me

Humiliation is a dramatic negative experience that distorts how we see ourselves. Over time, we become convinced that we're bad, inadequate, or worthless. Has this happened to you? Has the humiliation become such a defining point in your life that you've forgotten about your worth or the good that is in you? Greater self-compassion is not the only pathway to recovery from humiliation.

A second pathway to recovery is to reclaim your positive attributes and value to family, friends, work, and community. When people express appreciation, respect, and acceptance, we experience a boost in self-worth. But humiliation causes such an assault on our dignity and self-worth that we become numb to positive social feedback. Rebuilding your self-worth begins with greater attention to experiences of acceptance and positive recognition from others. The following exercise provides a diary for recording social experiences in which you are accepted, valued, and respected by others.

Exercise: Self-Worth Diary

Use the diary to write down daily experiences of being accepted, valued, or positively recognized by others. It might be a compliment, someone respectfully listening to your point of view, or a gesture that made you feel wanted and valued. Be specific when writing the example. It should include what was said or done by the person who made you feel wanted and valued. Most social interactions occur in certain areas of our life, so write the examples under the relevant life domain. Visit http://www.newharbinger .com/45052 to print copies of the Self-Worth Diary to keep handy so you can record positive experiences soon after they occur.

Life Domain	Experiences of Value, Worth, Recognition, and Success
Work & School	
Family & Intimate Relationships	
Friendships & Social Sphere	
Health & Physical Fitness	
Leisure & Recreation	
Community & Civic Activities	
Spiritual & Religious Faith	

After a few days, review your self-worth diary. Were you surprised at the number of times people important in your life expressed praise, recognition, and respect for your actions, opinions, knowledge, or character? Are you receiving more positive regard in some areas of your life than others? What do your diary entries tell you about your dignity, worth, and value as seen by others? If you had only a few diary entries, is it possible you are missing the positive input from others? You could feel so much hurt or be so demoralized by the humiliation that your brain is literally tuning out the recognition and respect of others. If this has happened to you, you'll need to spend more time collecting diary entries. You may also need the help of a therapist, friend, partner, or family member in recognizing the positive regard you receive in your daily life.

If you experienced multiple incidents of humiliation for an extended length of time, rebuilding your self-worth will take time. Martin experienced severe workplace bullying for years. When he finally quit and started a new job, his self-esteem was at an all-time low. He was convinced he was inferior to others, and he'd lost confidence in his work skills. It would take Martin many weeks (if not months) of writing in the Self-Worth Diary all the times he received the recognition and respect of his new managers and coworkers to undo the damage caused by past workplace bullying. For Martin, it was important to concentrate on capturing instances of positive regard in the work domain because that is where the humiliation took place. If your humiliation took place in a religious context, for example, you should focus on recording examples of recognition and respect within that life domain.

Possibly you're trying to rebuild your life after leaving an abusive intimate relationship. It is important to give yourself time and to diligently record experiences of love and respect if you are in a new relationship. You would use the family and intimate relationships category to record these experiences. Whatever domain is most relevant to you, a lot of effort is needed to recognize the respect and value of others. Unfortunately, it often takes three or four positives to counter the effects of one negative. The Self-Worth Diary is one tool you can use to retrain your mind to pay attention to the positive regard of others in your daily life. Over time, you'll be able to rebuild a sense of value and self-respect that was shattered by the effects of humiliation.

Wrap-Up

In this chapter you learned:

- Humiliation is a traumatic emotional experience involving undeserved ridicule, contempt, bullying, or degradation by someone with higher standing or authority.

- Persistent emotional pain and suffering as well as loss of dignity and self-worth are experienced by individuals who have repetitive negative thoughts and memories of the humiliation.

- The Humiliating Experiences Worksheet and the Humiliation Checklist can help you determine whether humiliation is an important factor in your emotional distress.

- Stopping humiliation must be the first step in recovery from emotional trauma.

- Learning to be kinder, more compassionate, and forgiving toward one's self through compassion-focused exercises is an important element in recovery from humiliation.

- Deliberate monitoring of positive regard and affirmation from others is a valuable approach to rebuilding self-worth, dignity, and respect.

What's Next?

Humiliation is the product of injustice, wrongdoing, and victimization. But humiliation is not the only emotion associated with injustice. Resentment is another negative emotion that can arise from feeling anger and bitterness over what we believe is wrongdoing by others. When resentment lingers in the form of repetitive negative thought, it can cause considerable unhappiness, distress, and irritability. Resentment is the final negative emotional state and is the focus of the last chapter in this workbook.

. . . . .

CHAPTER 8

Release from Resentment

Life is serious business! It is full of demands, responsibilities, challenges, and problems. It goes without saying that living in the twenty-first century is highly stressful for most people. The pressures on us are heightened by a competitive society where achievement, success, and status are taken as a measure of our worth. The only way to know where we stand is to compare ourselves with others. We all play this comparison game; it's as natural as breathing. But therein lies the rub! Comparing ourselves with others is risky because sometimes we conclude that the other person is doing better. And when we believe their success was due to an advantage they didn't deserve, resentment is the natural outcome. When resentment lingers, it can dominate our personality, so we become touchy, indignant, irritable, and angry. Does this describe you or someone you know? Do you compare yourself to others only to find they seem to be getting more breaks than you?

This is a chapter on resentment, and it begins with the story of Mya, who struggled with resentment that affected her most cherished relationships. We then delve into the main features of resentment that make it a difficult emotion to control. This is followed by assessment tools to determine whether resentment is contributing to your emotional distress. We conclude with two strategies that can relieve the stress of persistent resentment. One focuses on gratitude, and the other on forgiveness. Both may seem impossible to achieve when you've experienced unfair treatment, but they are essential to overcoming the negative effects of resentment.

Mya's Story: Filled with Resentment

Mya, a certified accountant and mother of two preschoolers, had a full but highly demanding lifestyle. Her fifteen-year marriage to Andrew, an investment advisor, was stable but somewhat stale given the demands of daily living. They were financially secure, had a few close friends, and were both healthy and physically fit. But over the years, Mya had changed from a relatively happy, easy-go-lucky university student to a serious, rather gloomy and cynical person. She felt on edge much of the time and realized she had become much more irritable at home and at work. She had frequent emotional outbursts that left her feeling ashamed and upset with her poor self-control. Mya wondered if she was slipping into a depression, but what others saw was an irritable, angry woman.

At work, Mya often complained that she was treated unfairly, that she was snubbed by her close friends, or that Andrew was taking her for granted. It seemed like her coworkers were getting perks and she was being overlooked. She failed to get promotions but blamed this on lacking the right demographic characteristics. To make matters worse, her ageing parents were becoming increasingly dependent on her but still favored her younger sister. Even her own children, whom she adored, were a source of annoyance. She was left doing a lot of the routine care while Andrew was free to do fun activities with them. It was clear they preferred their father over her. In all her interactions at home, at work, and in the community, Mya could only see injustice and unfairness.

Over the years, the experiences of perceived wrongdoing left a trail of resentment. Long ago as the unfavored daughter, Mya came to resent her younger sister. These experiences laid the groundwork for a belief that life is full of inequality and injustice, and so you have to "watch your back." The roles of mother, career woman, and spouse offered more opportunities for resentment. It came to dominate her outlook on life and her interactions with others. It caused tense and sometimes heated interactions at work, and it was creating more stress at home. She was being seen by others as difficult, touchy, and on edge. There was always some conflict or high drama in her life. But most of all, the resentment was causing considerable personal distress. Mya was becoming more anxious and despondent, and she didn't know why. On the surface, Mya was leading a successful life, but internally she felt frustrated, hurt, and upset. Why couldn't she be happier, more satisfied, content, and at peace with herself? For Mya, the roadblock to greater life satisfaction was resentment.

From Resentment to Resentful

Resentment is the feeling of displeasure, annoyance, or even anger toward someone we think has gained an undeserved advantage that causes us injury, hurt, or a sense of deprivation. It is considered one of the *moral emotions*, like shame, because it deals with what we think is right versus wrong or what should have or ought to have taken place. Resentment focuses on the behavior and characteristics we see in others. When resentment takes over, we can get so focused on the wrong or unfairness in others that we can't see the distortions in our own thinking. The negative consequences of resentment are not surprising. Persistent resentment is associated with anger, envy, and *schadenfreude* (taking pleasure in the misfortune of others; Feather and Sherman 2002).

In the moment, resentment can give us a false feeling of strength because we think we're standing up for what is right and just. We think of ourselves as wise and skeptical, making sure we don't fall victim to the injustice in this world (Enright 2017). This is one reason why resentment can become a way of thinking about others. When this cynical attitude sets in, we fall prey to a resentful way of thinking.

Mya's resentment got a big boost from the circumstances surrounding her hiring. A couple of other accountants were brought in to the firm along with Mya. Naturally, she was quite competitive with these other accountants and became increasingly preoccupied with how they were treated by the senior accountants and partners. She started keeping a mental tally of the perks and advantages they were getting, which seemed to far outnumber any breaks that came her way. At first, this made her feel more aware and assertive at work. But Mya's resentment toward these fellow accountants grew as she became convinced that they were being favored. In her mind, they didn't deserve it. Thoughts about not being recognized or valued grew in frequency, intensity, and uncontrollability. It all became almost unbearable when one of these accountants (Susan) got a promotion that Mya believed she deserved. It poisoned her attitude at work and was spilling over into her home life. Mya was spending too much time wrapped in repetitive negative thinking about the unfairness at the office. It was turning her into a resentful person—a jealous, angry, and spiteful woman she found loathsome.

Like Mya, resentment may have crept into your life, and you're wondering how you got to this point. Maybe you look back on earlier times when you had a more positive and accepting attitude toward life and the fortunes of others. But you've experienced unfairness in the intervening years, so now resentment has put a strain on your life satisfaction and emotional well-being. Before you can deal more effectively with resentment, you'll need a better understanding of its key features.

- *A desired outcome.* Resentment begins with an opportunity or outcome we desire for ourselves. It must be a highly valued outcome that's important to our self-worth. It could be something tangible like a job promotion, buying your dream home, taking an expensive vacation, and so forth. Or the desired outcome could be less tangible, like receiving the approval and acceptance of significant others, being recognized by influential people, being well liked and popular, or being considered an influential, successful person. Mya greatly desired career success because it made her feel like a valued person.

- *Disliked person receives the desired outcome.* When a desired outcome or succcess is achieved by a person we dislike, resentment is greater than if we liked the person (Pietraszkiewicz and Wojciszke 2014). If a person we like is successful, we're more likely to think he or she deserves it. If we don't like the individual, we're likely to think the success was undeserved or obtained unfairly. Mya disliked Susan, a fellow accountant of similar age and job experience. Whenever Susan was recognized, Mya could feel resentment build. She got along much better with Rachel, and though she was rising more quickly, it didn't bother Mya. Who are the people you dislike? Is your resentment more intense when these people have success?

- *Undeserved judgment.* Resentment is more intense when we believe the disliked person didn't deserve their success (Feather and Sherman 2002). We can argue that it's not right or fair they got the advantage or desired outcome. But our judgment of fairness is highly subjective. There's rarely an objective standard, so lots of people may disagree with you about whether the person deserved their success. Undeservedness judgments not only cause resentment but also the more extreme state of schadenfreude (Feather and Sherman 2002). None of us wants to admit to taking pleasure in the misfortune of others, but this is exactly where resentment takes us when we're consumed with judging whether people deserve their successes or not.

  Mya didn't believe her younger sister deserved their parents' praise and adoration because she lived on the other side of the country and wasn't availabe to help with their day-to-day support. Many families realize that parental love and appreciation are unconditional and do not depend on how much you do for the parent. So they would not agree with Mya that her sister did not deserve the adoration of her parents. Do you often think that people get more success or advantage than they deserve? Are you often judging situations in terms of fairness, justice, and what ought to have happened? If so, you could be more susceptible to resentment.

- *Controllability.* If a person receives a desired outcome that was uncontrollable, such as winning the lottery, we don't feel resentment. We might feel envy, but not resentment or anger. These emotions only occur when we believe the situation was under someone's control. Mya felt resentment when Susan got a promotion. She viewed the promotion as controllable because the senior partners could have made a different decision.

- *Unfairness.* Resentment will be especially strong if we believe we've been treated unfairly. If this happens repeatedly, we begin to see ourselves as a victim. Again, unfairness is a personal judgment that may not be shared by others. It can be difficult to determine whether you've been discriminated against or treated unjustly. Discrimination, prejudice, and injustice are all too common in our society, so it's simplistic to assume you're never being treated unfairly. But determining whether the unfairness is a feeling or a fact is not straighforward. It will require some type of external standard, such as determining whether your treatment was consistent with the company's policies and procedures for hiring and promotion. At other times, a tribunal may be needed to determine whether you were treated unfairly. Unfortunately, we often can't appeal to some external source, and so we are left to our own way of thinking. When that perspective includes a judgment of unfairness, resentment is often the consequence.

- *Repetitive negative thoughts (RNT).* With the previous processes in place, the seeds are now sown for a harvest of resentment. But what really drives the entire process toward an unhealthy form of resentment is the presence of RNT. Thinking repeatedly about the other person receiving an advantage or success you desired, how that person didn't deserve the success, and how unfairly you were treated throughout the ordeal will bring you back to resentment over and over again. Eventually, your preoccupation with these incidents will cloud your outlook and taint your social interactions. You'll become an angry person, and resentment will become your dominant emotion. You'll develop a heigthened sensitivity to injustice and inequity and believe that most people don't deserve their successes. You may become distrustful, cynical, argumentative, and complaining. You never wanted this, but you've become resentful, all fueled by repetitive negative thinking about the unfairness of life and the successes that others deserved less than you.

Figure 8.1 summarizes the key features involved in the pathway to resentment. You'll notice that RNT is the main conduit through which these processes build up feelings of resentment.

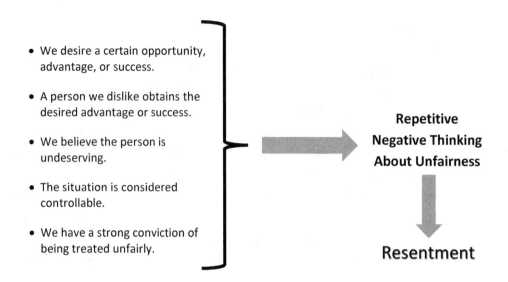

Figure 8.1. The Evolution of Persistent Resentment

Assessing Resentment

Resentment is more easily seen in others than in ourselves. Often other people see it in us before we see it ourselves. Resentment is a negative emotion we don't like to admit, so we're inclined to downplay its relevance. It's rare for a person to discover their resentment without help from family, close friends, or coworkers. This makes self-assessment of resentfulness more difficult than the other emotions covered in this workbook. The next exercise lists a few key questions that can help you determine whether resentment is playing a role in your distress.

Exercise: Resentful Experiences

The following questions refer to experiences that are relevant to resentment. Write your answers in the spaces provided.

1. Have you failed to obtain an important advantage, opportunity, or success because of unfair treatment? If so, briefly describe the experience(s).

    a. _____

    b. _____

c. _____

2. Did someone you know receive the desired outcome instead of you? Do you think this person deserved the success or opportunity? Briefly explain why the person was undeserving.

a. _____

b. _____

c. _____

3. Does the undeserving person make you feel hurt, irritated, or uncomfortable? Do you try to avoid this person? Are you overly sesnsitive or touchy about this person? If so, briefly describe some recent interactions.

a. _____

b. _____

c. _____

If you have had experiences relevant to the previous questions, then the conditions are right for feeling resentment. Thinking of these experiences in terms of desired outcome, fairness, and undeservedness can lead to resentment. On the other hand, if you found these questions irrelevant, then it's unlikely that resentment is a reason for your emotional distress.

Having experiences that are relevant to resentment is one thing, but being resentful is something different. The next exercise provides a checklist that assesses whether resentment is a significant personal problem. The checklist items focus on your response to the situations, thoughts, and feelings associated with resentment.

Exercise: The Resentment Checklist

The following checklist refers to thoughts, feelings, and experiences related to resentment and anger. Use the three-point rating scale to indicate how much each statement applies to you.

Statement	0 Doesn't Apply to Me	1 Applies to Me a Little	2 Applies to Me a Lot
1. I'm more likely to see injustice and unfairness in my world than other people.			
2. I am quite competitive, often comparing myself to other people.			
3. I am quick to take things personally.			
4. I have a strong sense of right and wrong as well as what ought or should happen in our actions and decisions toward others.			
5. I am highly motivated to succeed, to achieve personally valued goals and aspirations.			
6. I believe I've been treated more unfairly than the people I know.			
7. I've noticed that people who are often succesful don't deserve it or are given advantages that they don't deserve.			
8. I often think that I am not appreciated or valued by people important in my life.			
9. I often feel irritated and angry that others are getting more advantages than me.			
10. I find it hard to rejoice in the successes of other people.			
11. I can get stuck thinking over and over about someone else getting an advantage that I deserved more than that person.			

Statement	0 Doesn't Apply to Me	1 Applies to Me a Little	2 Applies to Me a Lot
12. I often think about how decisions could have been made differently so that I got the success rather than another person.			
13. I admit that I've taken delight when someone I dislike fails.			
14. I have a rather cynical worldview; I assume people are selfish and uncaring.			
15. I often complain about being treated badly.			
16. People probably find me "touchy" and somewhat defensive.			
17. I often think about being cheated out of opportunities or successes.			
18. There are successful people in my life whom I dislike but I still end up comparing myself to them.			

If you checked 1 or 2 for more than nine items, you might be struggling with resentment. The checklist is a new instrument developed for this workbook, so its accuracy needs to be researched. In the meantime, use it as a rough measure of problematic resentment and its effects on your relationships with others. If you endorsed only a few items, resentment may not be a relevant emotion for you.

There are several experiences that Mya could have recorded on the Resentful Experiences worksheet. Many of these experiences focused on work and the disappointment she felt with her stalled career. She firmly believed the senior partners didn't like her and instead favored Susan. She easily recounted occasions when her hard work went unrecognized and when she was unfairly overlooked for promotion or salary increases. She was convinced Susan was not outstanding in any way and so didn't deserve all the positive attention she was getting. Mya believed that Susan's only asset was her outgoing, flirtatious, and manipulative manner, which gave her a solid edge with the senior male partners. The more Mya thought about what was happening in the office, the more irritated and angry she felt toward these silly men and how easily Susan could manipulate them. She tried to avoid Susan as much as possible but found herself frequently gossiping about office politics. She felt like her true feelings of resentment were beginning to show at the office, and this bothered her. Mya liked to think she had better control over her emotions, that she could keep her true feelings to herself. But resentment was showing through, and it bothered her greatly.

Confronting Your Resentment

It's an insult to be considered resentful, so it's understandable that most people struggle to recognize its relevance in their life. We are aware of our anger, irritability, and low frustration tolerance, but we have a hard time seeing the resentment that's causing these negative emotions. If you often feel angry and irritated, consider whether resentment is a problem.

Maybe you completed the assessment exercises and you've concluded that resentment is a problem. If so, I commend you for insight, honesty, and willingness to face an undesirable characteristic in yourself. It takes courage to admit that we struggle with something as ugly as resentment. Admitting to a negative personality feature is the most important step toward healing and wholeness from resentment. Alternatively, the assessment exercises may have left you doubting, wondering whether resentment is the reason you so often struggle with negativity, anger, envy, and jealousy. Seeking the opinion of someone who knows you well—whose opinion you respect and you're able to accept—can be helpful. Remember that others can see our resentment before we see it ourselves.

If you've admitted to resentment, then you're ready to start work on it. Gratitude and forgiveness are two approaches that can transform how you deal with resentment. But to use them effectively, you'll first need to confront resentment and admit that it's a problem in your life.

Gratitude

Think of gratitude as the opposite of resentment. It involves a state of thankfulness characterized by appreciation for a favor or benefit you received from someone. People who are grateful believe they are sufficient in life, they appreciate the simple pleasures in life, and they easily recognize how their life has been enriched by others. They are able to see they've been given a positive outcome or advantage by others, and can express their appreciation for this benefit. Gratefulness contributes to happiness, life satisfaction, positive emotions, and better social relationships (Dickens 2017).

The grateful person has a positive, appreciative orientation to life. This is very different from the negative, cyncial attitude of resentfulness. The contrast is most evident in the main characteristics of each state.

Resentment	Gratitude
• Focus on injustice, unfairness, and mistreatment by others	• Focus on favorable, benefical treatment by others
• Judge others as gaining undeserved benefit over self	• Judge others as kind and benevolent toward self
• Bitter and envious of other's benefits; view their gain as your loss	• Take delight in the success of others; appreciate their contribution to your gain
• Heightened self-focus and entitlement	• Greater empathy and humility
• Negative, suspicious, and critical worldview	• Positive, accepting, and inclusive worldview

Resentment is a negative orientation that increases emotional distress, whereas gratitude improves positive emotion and well-being. This makes gratitude one of the most powerful strategies for dialing down resentment. But shifting from resentment to gratitude is a huge challenge. It takes determination and effort to learn the practice of gratitude. But there is good news. People can learn gratefulness and experience greater well-being by using *gratitude interventions* (Dickens 2017). Below you'll find a two-step approach for expressing gratefulness when having RNTs of resentment.

Exercise: Taking Stock of Resentment

Work on resentment starts by reevaluating your resentment experiences. Go back to the Resentful Experiences worksheet and answer the following three questions. Focus on the experience that you think about the most. If you have several important resentful experiences, use a blank sheet of paper to answer the three questions for each experience.

1. Write out an alternative possibility for understanding the resentful experience. Imagine an observer sees what happened to you. How might the observer conclude there was no unfair treatment toward you or the person you resent actually deserved their success?

    _____

    _____

    _____

2. Has resentment been costly? Make a list of its negative effects on you, your relationships, and your ability to live a productive and satisfying life.

a.	d.
b.	e.
c.	f.

3. If all things were possible, how could you correct the situation so you were treated fairly and the person you resent got what you think they deserved?

    _____

    _____

    _____

    _____

Were you able to complete the exercise and see your resentful experiences differently? First you were asked to compose a different perspective on the resentful experience. Then you listed all the negative consequences of being resentful. And finally you were challenged to think realistically about whether there is anything you can do now about the resented experience. From your answers, can you now see the futililty in being resentful? Are you now readly to abandon resentment as an unhealthy reaction to disappointment, loss, and failure? If you were unable to answer the questions, consider working with a friend, partner, or your therapist. You may be so stuck in the resentment perspective that it is impossible to see the situation differently without help.

Mya often felt annoyed with her close friends. She suspected they preferred each other and rarely took her interests into account. It seemed like she was often invited at the last minute, which caused her to feel considerable resentment. In response to the first question, Mya realized an observer might conclude that she was overly sensitive. The observer might recall the many occasions when Mya was included in a social activity and one of her other friends was not included. The observer might offer other explanations for why Mya is often invited at the last minute, such as having a more demanding job than the other women so they know her time is more limited. Rather than seeing it as a matter of unfairness, the alternative is she's being treated more fairly by her friends than she realizes.

In response to the second question, Mya could list many negative consequences of her friendship resentment, like (a) being more irritable and critical with her friends, (b) eroding their acceptance and desire to be around her, (c) decreasing her social attractiveness to others, (d) shrinking her friendship network and increasing her loneliness, and (e) decreasing her sense of value and worth. Mya would see from this list that she's paying a heavy price for her friendship resentment.

Mya might struggle to answer the third question, but eventually she'd realize there's nothing she can do to force her friends to treat her differently. Instead, she needs to take the initiative and invite them to social activities. Also, there is a greater advantage in assuming that years of friendship meant she was loved and valued by her friends. This was the assumption she would live out until her friends gave a clear and direct message that she was not wanted. It was time to abandon the grudge toward her friends and work on healing resentment with a more positive, grateful attitude.

Taking stock is the first step in recovery from resentment. You must be convinced that resentment is toxic and the experiences that seem so unfair can be seen differently. You'll need to be convinced there's nothing you can do about the past and that it's time to move on. If you can embrace the adage "it is what it is" when it comes to your resentful experiences, then you're ready for the next step in the healing process: learning the art of gratitude.

Exercise: The Gratitude Journal

Writing down your positive experiences in a gratitude journal is a key element in gratitude training. The more positive or desirable outcomes you record in your journal, the better. This should range from the trivial to the most significant, even life changing. Next, make note of the individuals or circumstances that made this positive outcome possible. You'll need to make multiple copies of this worksheet (available at http://www.newharbinger.com/45052) because the journal should be kept over several weeks.

Day	The Good Experiences, Positive Outcomes, Benefits, or Advantages You Received	The Circumstances or Person(s) That Caused This to Happen
Sunday		
Monday		
Tuesday		
Wednesday		
Thursday		
Friday		
Saturday		

Were you able to record at least one positive experience every day for which you could be grateful? No doubt there are many experiences that could be added to your Gratitude Journal, but you may be missing them because your attention is focused elsewhere. If you've been living with resentment for years, it will take a lot of practice to now focus your attention on positive experiences. You'll need to keep the Gratitude Journal over many weeks before you'll experience a shift in your attitude. If you're struggling to capture anything positive in your day, you may need the help of a friend, partner, or therapist to guide you in paying attention to the positive in your life.

For maximize effectiveness, the Gratitude Journal should become a mental health exercise you do daily. Try to make gratitude journaling a habit, like physical exercise. You wouldn't expect much health benefit by going to the gym once or twice. So it is with the Gratitude Journal. It needs to be kept daily over an extended period of time. But if making journal entries becomes a habit, you'll find it can have a powerful impact on resentment. This is because you're shifting from the negativity of resentment to the positive attitude of gratitude that contributes to personal well-being and happiness (Dickens 2017).

There is one other thing you can do to boost the power of gratitude. Practice expressing gratefulness to the individual(s) responsible for the good things you've written in your Gratitude Journal. Nothing helps more in creating a grateful attitude than backing it up with action. Actually telling someone how much you appreciate their kindness toward you will strengthen your investment in gratefulness.

Forgiveness

Did you find gratitude hard to practice? Now we come to a concept that's even more difficult for those with resentment: forgiveness. Forgiveness and mercy are old ideas that are foundational to many religious faiths. But there is new scientific evidence that forgiveness of those who treated you unfairly, who obtained favors and benefits at your expense, is a powerful way to work through resentment and restore emotional health (Enright and Fitzgibbons 2015). Forgiveness is not for the faint of heart. It's a long, difficult, and challenging process that can take months or even years. You can't simply decide one day to forgive and immediately transform your attitude toward the person you resent. But there are a few steps you can take toward that ultimate goal of forgiveness.

Exercise: The Hurt Letter

It's natural to feel hurt when someone treated you unfairly. The forgiveness process begins with an exercise designed to help you work through your hurt by using your imagination. Compose a ten- to fifteen-line letter in which you openly and honestly imagine telling the resented person how much you've been hurt by their wrongdoing or unfair treatment toward you. Write the letter in the present tense to indicate that you are still feeling hurt. Once you've written your hurt letter, schedule twenty-minute sessions several times a week to imagine reading the letter with great conviction and emotion to the resented person. [The hurt letter is for personal use only. It's not advisable to share the letter with the person you resent unless directed by your therapist.] You may want to change or add to the letter each time you imagine reading it. Your letter should contain the following points:

- A description of how the resented person hurt you

- The intensity and duration of the hurt

- The negative effects their wrongdoing or unfairness is having on your life and emotional well-being

- Why you don't deserve this unfair treatment

- Why you think the resented person doesn't deserve their success or benefit

- What the resented person can do to make things right for you

Use this space to write your hurt letter. If you need more space, use additional blank sheets of paper.

_____

_____

_____

_____

_____

_____

_____

Were you able to write about your hurt? Did you notice any change in your hurt after repeated imaginal sessions? Often our emotions soften when we repeatedly confront them, even in our imagination. As well, you may have discovered something new about your hurt. Maybe you've come to the conclusion that your hurt is an overreaction or that nothing can be done about the wrongdoing because it's all in the past. Possibly you can feel yourself coming closer to the point of letting go by working with your hurt letter.

If you've had difficulty with this exercise, take a look at a hurt letter Mya could write about Susan, who seems to be getting all the perks and advantages at work.

Susan, you have hurt me deeply in so many ways by your arrogant and entitled attitude. We both started work at the same time, but right from the start I could tell you looked down on me. There are so many times that you were critical of or embarrassed me in front of the senior partners [could include specific examples here]. I tried to be friendly, but you brushed me off. You are manipulative and flirtatious to get favors and promotions from the senior partners. I worked much harder than you, but this was never recognized because you always shone brighter in their eyes. For years I've left work distraught, discouraged, and feeling devalued. It's caused me to doubt my competence and whether I'll ever amount to anything in my career. I've become irritable, tense, and impatient at home. I know you're not smarter than me or a better accountant, but you know how to get what you want and crush anyone who gets in your way. I don't deserve to be pushed aside like this. I want you to stop being so selfish, entitled, and uncaring, and to treat me with respect and dignity.

Confronting your hurt might be the easiest part of the forgiveness process. The next step is more difficult. In order to forgive, it's necessary to see things from the perspective of the resented person. When we do this, we're better able to express understanding, mercy, and compassion toward that person. Use the following exercise to work on changing how you think about the resented person.

Exercise: Achieving Transcedence

We easily get stuck in our own view of a situation when feeling angry, hurt, or resentful. Transcedence involves rising above our point of view and adopting that of the person we resent. This is you, the one who's been hurt, trying to walk in the shoes of the person who wronged you. This requires a huge attitude shift. You may have the moral right to be angry or hurt, but you are choosing to abandon that right in order to forgive (Enright and Fitzgibbons 2015). The process of achieving this transcendent understanding involves two steps.

Step 1. Write a detailed account of three incidents of significant wrongdoing or unfair treatment you experienced from the resented person (review the Resentful Experiences worksheet). Describe exactly what happened, the circumstances, who was present, how you responded, and how it made you feel.

Incident #1: _____

_____

_____

Incident #2: _____

_____

_____

Incident #3: _____

_____

_____

Step 2. For each incident, imagine you're the resented person who treated you unfairly. Use your imagination to become the resented person. The following questions will help with this imagery exercise.

- What caused the resented person to act this way toward you?

- Was the unfair treatment intended to hurt you, or was the hurt more concidential?

- How does the resented person see you? How could you be a problem for this person?

- Did the resented person realize the negative effects of their behavior?

- Are there personal issues or difficult life circumstances that contributed to the resented person's unfair treatment?

Now, write a more understanding, merciful, and compassionate view of the resented person's unfair treatment.

Transcendent view of incident #1: _____

_____

_____

Transcendent view of incident #2: _____

_____

_____

Transcendent view of incident #3: _____

_____

_____

Once you've written a description of each incident from the resented person's perspective (the transcendent view), practice imagining yourself as the resented person in each of these incidents several times a week. With time, you'll notice a gradual shift in your attitude toward the resented person. This exercise will help you develop a more forgiving attitude toward the resented person. It is also important to write down current experiences that reinforce your more compassionate and forgiving view of the resented individual. Is there evidence this person is not quite as bad as you've been thinking?

Mya's anger and resentment toward Susan had deepened so much that she couldn't see any redeemable quality in her. But as she started to work on understanding incidents from Susan's perspective, she could feel herself soften toward a person who deserved much less than she got. Mya realized that Susan had entered the profession late and was trying to make up for lost time. She had separated from an abusive partner and was now trying to raise two children as a single parent. These life experiences had made her more self-reliant, competitive, and mistrustful. She was determined never to let anyone take advantage of her, and she probably considered Mya a threat to her success. Although Susan's rudeness and unfair treatment of Mya cannot be justified, Mya was able to be more forgiving when she thought of things from Susan's perspective.

To experience the healing effects of forgiveness, it is not enough to simply think differently about the resented person. It is also important to change your behavior. No doubt resentment and bitterness may have caused you to ignore, belittle, criticize, be argumentative, or even be combative toward the person you resent. The final exercise in the forgiveness process examines how you can act in a kinder, more compassionate, and merciful manner toward the resented person.

Exercise: Acts of Mercy

Below is a checklist of several negative interpersonal behaviors. Check the behaviors that describe how you've interacted with the resented person.

☐ Ignore	☐ Gossip	☐ Delight in their losses, defeats, or failures
☐ Argue	☐ Interrupt	☐ Try to embarrass them, put them down
☐ Criticize	☐ Raise voice, yell	☐ Be dishonest, deceptive
☐ Seek revenge	☐ Disagree	☐ Undermine
☐ Avoid	☐ Belittle	☐ Be aggressive
☐ Do not give eye contact	☐ Complain about	☐ Be demanding

Next, review the items you've checked and think about how you could act differently. What is a more thoughtful, compassionate, and merciful way to act toward the resented person? Despite not deserving this better treatment, how can you treat this individual as if you'd forgiven them? How could you express mercy, which means showing compassion toward someone who's offended you? Mercy begins with treating the resented person in a more positive, respectful, and affirmative manner. List four or five ways you could express positive interaction that would be opposite to the checked items.

Positive interaction #1: _____

Positive interaction #2: _____

Positive interaction #3: _____

Positive interaction #4: _____

Positive interaction #5: _____

The final step in this exercise is to engage in these positive interactions with the resented person. This involves acting out your forgiving attitude in your interactions with the resented individual. This will require tremendous effort and determination, especially if you're trying to correct years of negative interaction. You'll find it most helpful if you keep a journal of your positive interactions. This is a good way to motivate yourself and encourage the behavioral changes you are trying to make.

Forgiveness is a process that takes time and must be done at your own pace. Like gratitude, forgiveness requires a shift in attitude and life perspective. Resentment, anger, and bitterness focus on loss, unfairness, and often revenge. It can take a personal toll, especially if you're caught in persistent negative thinking about experiences of unfair treatment. Gratitude and forgiveness are effective approaches that can release you from the grip of resentment and help you refocus on cherished values and aspirations.

Wrap-Up

In this chapter you learned:

- Resentment leads to anger. It happens when we repeatedly think we've been treated unfairly in which an undeserving person gained a benefit that causes personal loss or injury.

- Resentment is a product of life circumstances and interactions with others. The Resentful Experiences and Resentment Checklist are assessment tools for determining whether you're stuck in repetitive thoughts and feelings of resentment.

- Gratitude training is an effective way to counter the emotional distress caused by persistently thinking about experiences of unfair treatment.

- Forgiveness is the most potent antidote to resentment. It requires a deeper understanding of the resented person and the practice of compassion and mercy. It's a multistep process that takes time, effort, and commitment. But forgiveness is a lifelong pursuit that is never fully realized. It's the commitment to forgive that may be the most critical element in achiving release from resentment.

Conclusion

Congratulations on making it to the finish line. At times it may have felt like a long-distance race or an extended workout at the gym. The topics we covered—worry, rumination, regret, shame, humiliation, and resentment—are stubborn, heartbreaking conditions that can have far-reaching effects on daily living. Our natural inclination is to avoid uncomfortable feelings. It takes insight, determination, and, yes, courage to pick up a workbook on disturbing thoughts and feelings. If you did the workbook exercises, I doubly commend you for taking such an active approach to overcoming emotional distress. Your commitment to get the most from the workbook is a testament to your strength and resourcefulness.

Let's take a moment to review some of the main themes of the workbook. We start with our most basic idea: the way we think affects the way we feel. Repetitive negative thoughts (RNT) make a significant contribution to persistent distress, like anxiety, depression, guilt, anger, and shame. RNT is unwanted, repetitive, and uncontrollable negative thinking that responds best to disengagement strategies. These strategies emphasize a more passive, accepting approach to the unwanted repetitive thoughts, a refocusing on the present moment, and giving up direct mental control. Disengagement strategies for RNT about the future (worry) focus on problem solving and decatastrophizing, whereas strategies for RNT based on the past (rumination) emphasize goal reorientation, replacing "why" with "how," and behavioral distraction. For regret, disengagement involves accepting that a failed decision may be forever lost and replacing it with an alternative plan that enables progress toward a core personal value. As well, overcoming regret involves rediscovering the reasons for a past poor decision. Shame and humiliation are moral emotions best overcome by adopting a narrower, more realistic perspective on the scope of their negative effects and learning to confront rather than avoid their triggers. Finally, gratitude and forgiveness are the most effective disengagement strategies for repetitive thoughts and feelings of resentment.

Doing self-help on our negative emotions takes an extra level of understanding, motivation, and perseverance. By getting to the end of this workbook, you've taken a major step toward healing and wholeness. I trust you've learned how to tackle your persistent distress more effectively, but your work is not finished. Completing the workbook is the beginning, but it is application that counts most. RNT is persistent, and it will continue to play havoc with your emotions and daily living. You'll want to come back to the relevant chapters time and again. Many of the strategies are skills that need to be practiced. You'll encounter new situations that'll require some tweaking of the strategies to improve their effectiveness. And disengagement strategies take time to master. The more you use them, the better you'll get at correcting unhelpful repetitive thinking. It goes without saying: life is a journey, if not a marathon. We all encounter new challenges and difficulties along the way. It's my wish that the time you've spent with this workbook has given you new tools to deal with your unwanted and distressing repetitive negative thoughts and feelings.

Acknowledgments

The idea for a workbook on repetitive negative thoughts started with an enthusiastic email I received from Wendy Millstine at New Harbinger Publications. I had previously written a workbook on negative intrusive thoughts called *The Anxious Thoughts Workbook*. Wendy noted that unwanted negative thoughts of emotional disorders also keep returning again and again, as if the depressed or anxious person was "addicted" to this way of thinking. It was a compelling observation, and when I looked further into the research literature, I found a fairly recent transdiagnostic category of negative thinking called *repetitive negative thought*. So, I am grateful to Wendy for creating the spark that culminated in this workbook. But the development of *The Negative Thoughts Workbook* wouldn't have been possible without the unwavering support, encouragement, and helpful advice of Ryan Buresh, my acquisitions editor at New Harbinger. I am so grateful to Ryan and Clancy Drake, who provided valuable direction and suggestions not only on the communication style and organization of the manuscript but on key substantive issues as well.

The information and treatment strategies presented in this workbook wouldn't be possible without the pioneering research of several prominent psychologists, including Thomas Ehring, Susan Nolen-Hoeksema, Suzanne Segerstrom, and Edward Watkins. Other prominent researchers and clinicians contributed knowledge and treatment insights critical to the treatment of repetitive thoughts. These include Aaron T. Beck, Thomas Borkovec, Michel Dugas, Martin Enright, Paul Gilbert, Daniel Wegner, and Adrian Wells. I owe a huge debt to one of the great pioneers of CBT, Dr. Aaron T. Beck, whom I am honored to know as my mentor, friend, and coauthor. His ideas permeate through every page of this workbook. Others I count as friends and colleagues include Judy Beck, Robert Leahy, Christine Purdon, Adam Radomsky, and John Riskind, with whom I've benefited from many hours of inspiring conversations over the years. But I am especially grateful to the hundreds of patients I've seen in my practice. I have learned most from them sharing their most private struggles with disturbing repetitive thoughts and feelings. I continue to appreciate the wise counsel of my agent, Bob Diforio, who has been so generous with his time, knowledge, and encouragement as well as his expertise and professionalism.

Last, but not least, I am most indebted to my partner of four decades, Nancy Nason-Clark, as well as my daughters, Natascha and Christina, who, together with their partners, Jaron and Sean, have endured my perfectionist strivings with the written word.

References

Beck, A. T., and G. Emery (with R. L. Greenberg). 1985. *Anxiety Disorders and Phobias: A Cognitive Perspective.* New York: Basic Books.

Borkovec, T. D., H. Hazlett-Stevens, and M. L. Diaz. 1999. "The Role of Positive Beliefs About Worry in Generalized Anxiety Disorder and Its Treatment." *Clinical Psychology and Psychotherapy* 6: 126–138.

Clark, D. A. 2018. *The Anxious Thoughts Workbook: Skills to Overcome the Unwanted Intrusive Thoughts That Drive Anxiety, Obsessions & Depression.* Oakland, CA: New Harbinger Publications.

Clark, D. A., and A. T. Beck. 2012. *The Anxiety and Worry Workbook: The Cognitive Behavioral Solution.* New York: Guilford Press.

Connolly, T., and M. Zeelenberg. 2002. "Regret in Decision Making." *Current Directions in Psychological Science* 11 (6): 212–216.

Dickens, L. R. 2017. "Using Gratitude to Promote Positive Change: A Series of Meta-Analyses Investigating the Effectiveness of Gratitude Interventions." *Basic and Applied Social Psychology* 39 (4): 193–208.

Dugas, M. J., and M. Robichaud. 2007. *Cognitive-Behavioral Treatment for Generalized Anxiety Disorder: From Science to Practice.* New York: Routledge.

Ehring, T., and E. R. Watkins. 2008. "Repetitive Negative Thinking as a Transdiagnostic Process." *International Journal of Cognitive Therapy* 1 (3): 192–205.

Ehring, T., U. Zetsche, K. Weidacker, K. Wahl, S., Schöenfeld, and A. Ehlers. 2011. "The Perseverative Thinking Questionnaire (PTQ): Validation of a Content-Independent Measure of

Repetitive Negative Thinking." *Journal of Behavior Therapy and Experimental Psychiatry* 42 (2): 225–232.

Elshout, M., R. M. A. Neilissen, and I. van Beest. 2017. "Conceptualising Humiliation." *Cognition and Emotion* 31 (8): 1581–1594.

Enright, R. 2017. "Why Resentment Lasts—and How to Defeat It." Retrieved from https://www .psychologytoday.com/us/blog/the-forgiving-life/201703/why-resentment-lasts-and-how -defeat-it on August 24, 2019.

Enright, R. D., and R. P. Fitzgibbons. 2015. *Forgiveness Therapy: An Empirical Guide for Resolving Anger and Restoring Hope.* Washington, DC: American Psychological Association.

Feather, N. T., and R. Sherman. 2002. "Envy, Resentment, *Schadenfreude,* and Sympathy: Reactions to Deserved and Undeserved Achievement and Subsequent Failure." *Personality and Social Psychology Bulletin* 28 (7): 953–961.

Gilbert, P. 1997. "The Evolution of Social Attractiveness and Its Role in Shame, Humiliation, Guilt, and Therapy." *British Journal of Medical Psychology* 70 (2): 113–147.

Gilbert, P. 2009. *The Compassionate Mind: A New Approach to Life's Challenges.* Oakland, CA: New Harbinger Publications.

Gilovich, T. 1995. "The Experience of Regret: What, When, and Why." *Psychological Review* 102 (2): 379–395.

Gonçalves, D. C., and G. J. Byrne. 2013. "Who Worries Most? Worry Prevalence and Patterns Across the Lifespan." *International Journal of Geriatric Psychiatry* 28: 41–49.

Hartling, L. M., and T. Luchetta. 1999. "Humiliation: Assessing the Impact of Derision, Degradation, and Debasement." *The Journal of Primary Prevention* 19 (4): 259–278.

Klein, D. C. 1991. "The Humiliation Dynamic: An Overview." *The Journal of Primary Prevention* 12 (2): 93–121.

Kraines, M. A., C. P. Krug, and T. T. Wells. 2017. "Decision Justification Theory in Depression: Regret and Self-Blame." *Cognitive Therapy and Research* 41: 556–561.

Krott, N. R., and G. Oettingen. 2018. "Mental Contrasting of Counterfactual Fantasies Attenuates Disappointment, Regret, and Resentment." *Motivation and Emotion* 42: 17–36.

Leahy, R. L. 2005. *The Worry Cure: Seven Steps to Stop Worry from Stopping You.* New York: Harmony Books.

Leahy, R. L. 2015. *Emotional Schema Therapy.* New York: Guilford Press.

Levine, A. Z., and D. M. Warman. 2016. "Appraisals of and Recommendations for Managing Intrusive Thoughts: An Empirical Investigation." *Psychiatry Research* 245: 207–216.

Luban, D. 2009. "Human Dignity, Humiliation, and Torture." *Kennedy Institute of Ethics Journal* 19 (3): 211–230.

McEvoy, P. M., A. E. J. Mahoney, and M. L. Moulds. 2010. "Are Worry, Rumination, and Post-Event Processing One and the Same? Development of the Repetitive Thinking Questionnaire." *Journal of Anxiety Disorders* 24 (5): 509–519.

National Coalition Against Domestic Violence (NCADV). 2019. "National Statistics." Retrieved from https://www.speakcdn.com/assets/2497/domestic_violence2.pdf on July 21, 2019.

Neff, K. D. 2011. *Self-Compassion: Stop Beating Yourself Up and Leave Insecurity Behind.* New York: William Morrow.

Negrao, C., G. A. Bonanno, J. G. Nol, F. M. Putnam, and P. K. Trickett. 2005. "Shame, Humiliation, and Childhood Sexual Abuse: Distinct Contributions and Emotional Coherence." *Child Maltreatment* 10 (4): 350–363.

Nolen-Hoeksema, S. 1991. "Responses to Depression and Their Effects on the Durations of Depressive Episodes." *Journal of Abnormal Psychology* 100 (4): 569–582.

Pietraszkiewicz, A., and B. Wojciszke. 2014. "Joy, Schadenfreude, Sorrow, and Resentment as Responses Restoring Balance in Cognitive Units." *Social Psychology* 45 (4): 274–285.

Roese, N. J. 1997. "Counterfactual Thinking." *Psychological Bulletin* 121 (1): 133–148.

Roese, N. J., K. Epstude, F. Fessel, M. Morrison, R. Smallman, A. Summerville, and S. C. Segerstrom. 2009. "Repetitive Regret, Depression, and Anxiety: Findings from a Nationally Representative Sample." *Journal of Social and Clinical Psychology* 28 (6): 671–688.

Roese, N. J., and A. Summerville. 2005. "What We Regret Most…and Why." *Personality and Social Psychology Bulletin* 31 (9): 1273–1285.

Ruscio, A. M., L. S. Hallion, C. C. W. Lim, S. Aguilar-Gaxiola, A. Al-Hamzawi, J. Alonso, L. H. Andrade et al. 2017. "Cross-Sectional Comparison of the Epidemiology of *DSM-5* Generalized Anxiety Disorder Across the Globe." *Journal of the American Medical Association Psychiatry* 74 (5): 465–475.

Segerstrom, S. C., J. C. I. Tsao, L. E. Alden, and M. G. Craske. 2000. "Worry and Rumination: Repetitive Thought as a Concomitant and Predictor of Negative Mood." *Cognitive Therapy and Research* 24 (6): 671–688.

Tangney, J. P., and R. L. Dearing. 2002. *Emotions and Social Behavior.* New York: Guilford Press.

Tangney, J. P., R. S. Miller, L. Flicker, and D. H. Barlow. 1996. "Are Shame, Guilt, and Embarrassment Distinct Emotions?" *Journal of Personality and Social Psychology* 70 (6): 1256–1269.

Treynor, W., R. Gonzalez, and S. Nolen-Hoeksema. 2003. "Rumination Reconsidered: A Psychometric Analysis." *Cognitive Therapy and Research* 27 (3): 247–259.

Watkins, E. R. 2008. "Constructive and Unconstructive Repetitive Thought." *Psychological Bulletin* 134 (2): 163–206.

Watkins, E. R. 2016. *Rumination-Focused Cognitive-Behavioral Therapy for Depression.* New York: Guilford Press.

Wegner, D. M. 1994. *White Bears and Other Unwanted Thoughts: Suppression, Obsession, and the Psychology of Mental Control.* New York: Guilford Press.

Wegner, D. M. 2011. "Setting Free the Bears: Escape from Thought Suppression." *American Psychologist* 66 (8): 671–680.

Wells, A. 2009. *Metacognitive Therapy for Anxiety and Depression.* New York: Guilford Press.

Wells, A., and M. I. Davies. 1994. "The Thought Control Questionnaire: A Measure of Individual Differences in the Control of Unwanted Thoughts." *Behaviour Research and Therapy* 32 (8): 871–878.

Workplace Bullying Institute (WBI). 2017. "2017 WBI U.S. Workplace Bullying Survey." Retrieved from https://www.workplacebullying.org/multi/img/2017/Infographic-2017.png on July 21, 2019.

David A. Clark, PhD, is a clinical psychologist and professor emeritus at the University of New Brunswick. He is author or coauthor of several books on depression, anxiety, and obsessive-compulsive disorder (OCD), including *The Anxiety and Worry Workbook* with Aaron T. Beck (founder of cognitive therapy), *The Anxious Thoughts Workbook*, and *Cognitive-Behavioral Therapy for OCD and Its Subtypes*. Clark is a founding fellow and trainer consultant with the Academy of Cognitive and Behavioral Therapies, and fellow of the Canadian Psychological Association. He is author of the blog, *The Runaway Mind*, on www.psychologytoday.com.

Foreword writer **Robert L. Leahy, PhD**, is author or editor of twenty-seven books, including *The Worry Cure*, *The Jealousy Cure*, and *Beat the Blues*. He is director of the American Institute for Cognitive Therapy in New York, NY, and clinical professor of psychology at Weill Cornell Medical College. Leahy has been featured in *The New York Times*, *The Wall Street Journal*, and more.

MORE BOOKS from
NEW HARBINGER PUBLICATIONS

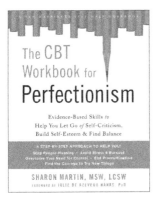
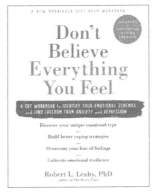

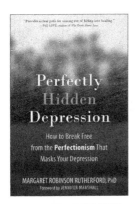
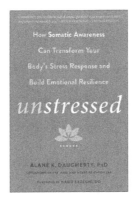
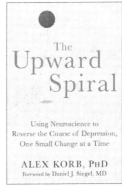

Register your **new harbinger** titles for additional benefits!

When you register your **new harbinger** title—purchased in any format, from any source—you get access to benefits like the following:

- Downloadable accessories like printable worksheets and extra content

- Instructional videos and audio files

- Information about updates, corrections, and new editions

Not every title has accessories, but we're adding new material all the time.

Access free accessories in 3 easy steps:

1. Sign in at NewHarbinger.com (or **register** to create an account).

2. Click on **register a book**. Search for your title and click the **register** button when it appears.

3. Click on the **book cover or title** to go to its details page. Click on **accessories** to view and access files.

That's all there is to it!

If you need help, visit:

NewHarbinger.com/accessories

new harbinger
CELEBRATING
40 YEARS